The Voice to Parliament

HANDBOOK

All the detail you need

Thomas Mayo & Kerry O'Brien

Cartoons by Cathy Wilcox
Design and infographics by Jenna Lee

Aboriginal and Torres Strait Islander peoples are advised that this publication contains the names of deceased people. Hardie Grant apologises for any distress this may inadvertently cause.

Hardie Grant

EXPLORE

Published in 2023 by Hardie Grant Explore, an imprint of Hardie Grant Publishing

Hardie Grant Explore (Melbourne)
Wurundjeri Country
Building 1, 658 Church Street
Richmond, Victoria 3121

Hardie Grant Explore (Sydney)
Gadigal Country
Level 7, 45 Jones Street
Ultimo, NSW 2007

www.hardiegrant.com/au/explore

A catalogue record for this book is available from the National Library of Australia

Hardie Grant acknowledges the Traditional Owners of the Country on which we work, the Wurundjeri People of the Kulin Nation and the Gadigal People of the Eora Nation, and recognises their continuing connection to the land, waters and culture. We pay our respects to their Elders past and present.

For all relevant publications, Hardie Grant Explore commissions a First Nations consultant to review relevant content and provide feedback to ensure suitable language and information is included in the final book. Hardie Grant Explore also includes traditional place names and acknowledges Traditional Owners, where possible, in both the text and mapping for their publications.

Traditional place names are included in palawa kani, the language of Tasmanian Aboriginal People, with thanks to the Tasmanian Aboriginal Centre.

The Voice to Parliament Handbook
ISBN 9781741178869

10 9 8 7 6 5 4

Publisher
Melissa Kayser
Editor
Bernadette Foley
Proofreader
Puddingburn Publishing Services
First Nations consultant
Jamil Tye, Yorta Yorta
Design and infographics
Jenna Lee
Production coordinator
Simone Wall

Typeset in Adobe Caslon Pro 11pt by Mike Kuszla
Colour reproduction by Splitting Image Colour Studio

Printed in Australia by Griffin Press.

Contents

The Uluru Statement from the Heart

We, gathered at the 2017 National Constitutional Convention, coming from all points of the southern sky, make this statement from the heart:

Our Aboriginal and Torres Strait Islander tribes were the first sovereign Nations of the Australian continent and its adjacent islands, and possessed it under our own laws and customs. This our ancestors did, according to the reckoning of our culture, from the Creation, according to the common law from 'time immemorial', and according to science more than 60,000 years ago.

This sovereignty is *a spiritual notion: the ancestral tie between the land, or 'mother nature', and the Aboriginal and Torres Strait Islander peoples who were born therefrom, remain attached thereto, and must one day return thither to be united with our ancestors. This link is the basis of the ownership of the soil, or better, of sovereignty.* It has never been ceded or extinguished, and co-exists with the sovereignty of the Crown.

How could it be otherwise? That peoples possessed a land for sixty millennia and this sacred link disappears from world history in merely the last two hundred years?

With substantive constitutional change and structural reform, we believe this ancient sovereignty can shine through as a fuller expression of Australia's nationhood.

Proportionally, we are the most incarcerated people on the planet. We are not an innately criminal people. Our children are aliened from their families at unprecedented rates. This cannot be because we have no love for them. And our youth languish in detention in obscene numbers. They should be our hope for the future.

These dimensions of our crisis tell plainly the structural nature of our problem. This is *the torment of our powerlessness.*

We seek constitutional reforms to empower our people and take *a rightful place* in our own country. When we have power over our destiny our children will flourish. They will walk in two worlds and their culture will be a gift to their country.

We call for the establishment of a First Nations Voice enshrined in the Constitution.

Makarrata is the culmination of our agenda: *the coming together after a struggle*. It captures our aspirations for a fair and truthful relationship with the people of Australia and a better future for our children based on justice and self-determination.

We seek a Makarrata Commission to supervise a process of agreement-making between governments and First Nations and truth-telling about our history.

In 1967 we were counted, in 2017 we seek to be heard. We leave base camp and start our trek across this vast country. We invite you to walk with us in a movement of the Australian people for a better future.

26 May 2017

The creation of the Uluṟu Statement from the Heart

THOMAS MAYO

The creation of the Uluṟu Statement from the Heart involved thousands of First Nations people from hundreds of Aboriginal and Torres Strait Islander communities and from a range of perspectives and experiences. The deliberations were conducted over many days, through Regional Dialogues that culminated at the Uluṟu National Constitutional Convention.

The Dialogues and the Convention were the most extensive, well-informed and well-formulated constitutional dialogues Indigenous peoples have ever had. They were proportionately more representative than the constitutional convention debates that led to the Australian Constitution in 1901, from which First Nations people were excluded.[1] The Dialogues sprang from a sixteen-member referendum council, backed in the spirit of bipartisanship by Prime Minister Malcolm Turnbull and Opposition Leader Bill Shorten, formed in December 2015 to advise the Government on a pathway to constitutional recognition.

The Uluṟu Dialogues were regional, covering the entire continent and adjacent islands, and the lands of all Indigenous First Nations. They were designed and led by First Nations experts and local leaders, with a commitment to achieving inclusion; the participants were invited in accordance with a formula that ensured representation for gender balance, Stolen Generations, youth and First Nations People Off Country. Also, Traditional Owners from each region were strongly represented.

Translators and experts in constitutional law were readily available at each Dialogue. The experts provided presentations about how the nation's political and legal systems work and the history of Indigenous advocacy. At the end of every Dialogue the participants endorsed an accurate record of the meeting. And finally, those who attended the meetings elected delegates to take those records to the culminating National Constitutional Convention. The delegates' job at the Convention was to synthesise the Dialogue outcomes, bringing together a national consensus position – one collective statement from First Nations people.

The priority in all regions and in the consensus reached at the Uluru National Constitutional Convention was to constitutionally enshrine a First Nations Voice to Parliament.

The Regional Dialogues

Hobart, 9–11 December 2016
Broome, 10–12 February 2017
Dubbo, 17–19 February 2017
Darwin, 22–24 February 2017
Perth, 3–5 March 2017
Sydney, 10–12 March 2017
Melbourne, 17–19 March 2017
Cairns, 24–26 March 2017
Ross River, 31 March–2 April 2017
Adelaide, 7–9 April 2017
Brisbane, 21–23 April 2017
Torres Strait, 5–7 May 2017
Canberra, 10 May 2017
Uluru National Constitutional Convention, 23–26 May 2017

What the Voice means to me

THOMAS MAYO

During the campaign for an Aboriginal and Torres Strait Islander Voice to Parliament, I have often sat on a tiny chair, my knees at my elbows, in a classroom surrounded by children. There are always a few who have the wriggles and giggles, but mostly they sit quietly, cross-legged, staring at the book I'm holding.

Usually, the children have already read *Finding Our Heart: A Story about the Uluru Statement for Young Australians*. Teachers and parents often tell me it is their children's favourite book, perhaps because of the illustrations by Archibald Prize winning artist Blak Douglas. Or maybe it's because the kids understand better than adults that it is *their* story told in its pages.

The children and youth of Australia seem to have an innate understanding that it is our Aboriginal and Torres Strait Islander culture and heritage that makes this country unique. Not wearing thongs, having a barbie, acting like a larrikin, mateship or hanging out at the beach. Although we can love all those things too.

As I read my book to children, I always stop at certain pages to discuss the words and the illustrations, and to ask them questions. On the page that reminds them that we come from many different nations, they tell me which flags they recognise, and some will mention which flags they notice are missing. When I reach the page with the AIATSIS map of the continent, showing the many First Nations that make up Aboriginal and Torres Strait Islander Australia, the children always know whose Country they are on; they raise their hands in the air, hoping to be the first to tell me. On the page with the image of the Uluṟu Statement from the Heart canvas, I point out the hundreds of names around the Statement, and I tell the children about the numerous Aṉangu stories in the surrounding artwork.

'What is the oldest thing in the world you can think of?' I ask.

'The pyramids', or 'castles', some might say.

Whatever they call out, I can confidently tell them, 'These Aboriginal stories are way, way, *waaaay* older than those things.' And they marvel at how ancient the stories are.

When I reach the final page of the book and ask them, 'Will you help find the heart of the nation?' – and by then they understand that the voices, culture and heritage of Aboriginal and Torres Strait Islander peoples help make up the heart of the nation – the children always say, 'YES!'

Occasionally, after reading the book, I invite children to write or draw a response to the Uluṟu Statement's invitation to recognise Indigenous peoples with a Voice to Parliament – to find the heart of the nation. The most wonderful, heart-warming, intelligent responses emerge on white pages that the children cover with colourful images and meaningful words.

Some write letters:

Dear Aboriginal people, if I could vote yes, I would. Your voices are important to finding the heart of our country so it can be better again.
– Peter, Launceston

Dear Prime Minister, saying yes to a Voice is a fair thing to do. When I am going to play a game with my friends, it is fair that we make the rules together before we play so we are all happy. Please listen to Aboriginal people.
– Sophie, Canberra

And some express themselves in art.[1]

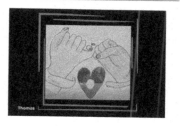
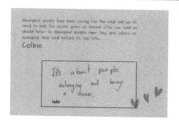

In those moments especially, often with a tear in my eye, I wish the children could vote. They are curious about difference, not prejudiced; eager to learn, rather than ignore.

They ask, 'Why haven't we given Indigenous peoples this Voice already?'

I believe it is up to us to answer their question with our actions now, in our generation. We should not pass on the burdens of our colonial past, nor a constitutional ignorance of our Indigenous heritage to our children, many of whom will become the future leaders of our great nation.

If we miss this opportunity, it will be generations before there is another chance.

ooooo

Australians have rarely agreed to change the Constitution because, as it is written, the Constitution has served most people quite well.

For Aboriginal and Torres Strait Islander peoples, though, the Constitution has long excluded us. From the earliest European settlement, we were forced into wars on our own lands, defending ourselves against massacres, the abduction of our children, slavery and all manner of cruelties.

The Constitution prohibited the counting of Indigenous peoples as citizens until the 1967 referendum, when the Australian people overwhelmingly voted 'Yes' to remove Section 127, titled 'Aborigines not to be counted in the reckoning of the population'; and to altering Section 51 (xxvi), or the 'race power', which had prohibited the federal government from using its power to make special laws for the 'Aboriginal race'.

The 1967 referendum was the most successful in Australia's history, with an overall 'Yes' vote of 91.8 per cent.

My father, a Kaurareg Aboriginal, Kalkalgal and Erubamle Torres Strait Islander man, was born before 1967. He was not counted as an Australian for most of his childhood. He and his parents lived under a government 'Protector' – a white man who had complete control over Indigenous peoples' lives. The government's authorities could exile my people from their homelands at any time. They withheld our wages. They could direct us to work without pay. My father and his siblings could have been stolen from their parents and relocated thousands of kilometres away, legally.

My Elders, therefore, have a deep understanding of why constitutional change is important. For all that we have owned that has been taken away, for all we have gained that has been destroyed, and although there have been many promises broken, the constitutional change made in 1967 has been consistent, untouched, regardless of who has been in government. We know that constitutional change is as close as we can get to lasting progress. For my children, I want progress that cannot be removed by a shift in policy. I want a Voice that cannot be repealed by a government that is avoiding accountability.

I believe Australians overwhelmingly supported the 1967 referendum because it was a question about fairness. Yet still today, the Constitution, though we are counted, does not recognise Indigenous peoples as the first peoples of Australia, nor does it ensure that when decisions are made about us, as a distinct people, that we have an opportunity to have a say.

ooooo

I will never forget when the Uluṟu Statement from the Heart was read for the first time on the morning of 26 May 2017. With raucous acclamation, we stood as one at the Uluṟu National Constitutional Convention, to endorse its words and its proposal to establish a constitutionally enshrined Aboriginal and Torres Strait Islander Voice.

The delegates came from urban centres, and rural and remote communities; we were Indigenous healers, service workers, labourers, tradespeople, cultural leaders, rangers – you name an occupation, region or First Nation and there was someone at the convention with that background.

To reach the consensus position, we suspended our disbelief that this modern nation could agree to meaningful constitutional change. After many days of discussion and debate, a great majority of the delegates chose unity and hope.

The hard work Indigenous peoples did should never be underestimated. No one should discount the emotional toil in the debates and discussions, nor how carefully we considered the lessons from the past so we might determine the path to a better future for all Australians.

To reach a collective position, we relied on our culture. We respected each other's various perspectives and we listened to each other. We practised reciprocity. And finally, we were willing to reach a compromise among ourselves so that we could stand with the strength of unity.

The Voice proposal is a wonderful consensus position, informed by history, experience and sound, logical sense.

We have continued to work hard. The Uluṟu Statement – the invitation to accept our Voice – is written to the Australian people. And so, we have taken the invitation to millions of Australians to let them know why we have invited them to walk with us.

This nation-building opportunity at a referendum is not a government idea. Rather, it is a gift from Indigenous peoples.

∞∞∞

Soon after the Uluṟu Constitutional Convention in 2017, I had the honour of carrying the sacred Uluṟu Statement canvas, signed by the 250 delegates and imbued with Aṉangu lore, to Australians all around the country and from all walks of life. When the Liberal government dismissed our proposal for a Voice in October that year, many Australians joined us by refusing to take 'No' for an answer.

The momentum we built, beginning with a uniquely national Indigenous consensus in the heart of the nation at Uluṟu, followed by an ongoing campaign, has convinced the current government to act. The Labor government has committed to asking the Australian people to decide. I hope the result will reflect the people's goodwill and propensity towards fairness.

∞∞∞

We cannot rely on goodwill alone, though. It is important for voters to understand that voting 'Yes' will benefit Indigenous peoples in a practical way, while also strengthening our democracy and our egalitarian society.

Finding ways to inform Australians to counter misinformation has been an important part of my work since the Uluṟu Statement was created six years ago. In addition to giving hundreds of speeches, I have used writing to inform people. This is my fourth book about the Uluṟu Statement from the Heart, though this one focuses on the Voice referendum.

Finding the Heart of the Nation was published in October 2019, a narrative series of interviews I conducted with twenty Aboriginal and Torres Strait Islander people about the many reasons why they support the Uluṟu Statement. *Finding Our Heart*, the children's book I mentioned earlier, was published in June 2020. And *Freedom Day*, a book that shares the Gurindji People's perspective on the importance of a Voice, co-authored with Gurindji leader Vincent Lingiari's granddaughter, Rosie Smiler, was published in August 2021.

Kerry O'Brien and I met when I launched my first book, *Finding the Heart of the Nation*. As you will read in these pages, Kerry is very well informed when it comes to Indigenous affairs. His intimate knowledge, much of it sourced from his interviews with prime ministers and some of the greatest Indigenous leaders, and his ABC reports over decades, led me to him when I had the idea to write this book. Kerry and I have come together to give you the detail you need to decide how you will vote in the referendum.

The referendum is imminent. On your ballot, you may only vote 'Yes' or 'No'. I believe it is a choice between Australia being a mature nation, unique in the world, with over 60 millennia of unbroken civilisation, or being a young nation at merely 122 years since Federation. It is a choice between improving the lives of Aboriginal and Torres Strait Islander peoples, through the simple act of asking the Parliament to listen, or choosing to accept more of the same.

As a signatory to the Uluru Statement from the Heart, I invite you to choose 'Yes'. Together, our country has much to gain.

What the Voice means to me

KERRY O'BRIEN

The Uluru Statement from the Heart is a remarkable landmark document – eloquent in the writing and generous in spirit – very consciously pitched as a conservative blueprint for genuine reconciliation.

It is remarkable because it emerged from a broad consensus with minimal dissent from the biggest ever meeting of Indigenous leaders about constitutional recognition. These 250 leaders represented hundreds of communities across the length and breadth of the nation. After decades of halting steps and outright failures by successive governments, the Uluru Statement takes us all a giant stride closer to genuine reconciliation.

Embodied in the Uluru Statement is a request for three fundamentally important but quite reasonable things. First among them is to have constitutional recognition of First Nations people. This would permanently ensure their right to have a Voice to the Australian Parliament and Executive Government when it is considering passing laws that will have an impact on them. Not a Voice *in* the Parliament, but a Voice making representations *to* the Parliament. It's been tried in the past, but without the clout of constitutional recognition it's been too easily sidelined.

The other two elements of the Uluṟu Statement are the process for truth-telling about Indigenous history and for agreement-making, the Makarrata. These elements, under the guidance of a Makarrata Commission, would not require constitutional change and would be created through an Act of Parliament. In other postcolonial democracies like ours around the world these are not radical concepts.

Representatives of the British Government signed the Treaty of Waitangi with 45 Māori chiefs in 1840, when Aotearoa New Zealand was still part of the colony of New South Wales. At that time, Indigenous peoples under the same colonial umbrella in Australia were rendered invisible through the now discredited device of *terra nullius*, 'land belonging to no one'. The treaty certainly didn't prevent discrimination in Aotearoa New Zealand, but it has led to a much healthier and more productive relationship between governments and Māori people over time, and it acknowledges a number of fundamental rights.

Canada has negotiated both historic and more recent treaties since 1975 with its First Nations people, some of which have facilitated land claims and some of which include the right to self-government. Canada also conducted a truth and reconciliation commission, which spent six years hearing testimonies from over 6000 people and releasing millions of government documents, making them publicly accessible. It has laid the basis for a better informed, more truthful record of Canada's history for future generations, and provided a solid, practical stepping stone to a more genuine reconciliation.[1]

There is one other remarkable thing about the Uluṟu Statement. It reflects a conscious choice by the largest representative body of First Nations leadership in our history to go beyond the politicians of this country and appeal directly to the people. To all of us.

The politicians have had their chance over many decades to close the yawning gaps of inequality and to lead us on a pathway from conflict to reconciliation, and their success has been incremental.

Australia has nothing to lose and a great deal to gain by voting 'Yes' in the Voice referendum. One key reason why Indigenous policy has failed so fundamentally at times is because it has been written and implemented from Canberra by non-Indigenous politicians and bureaucrats, without listening to the people they're supposed to be helping.

There have been many Indigenous voices seeking to advise governments on community needs over decades but they have never been supported with any consistency, while the yawning equity gap between Indigenous peoples and the rest of us remains. A Voice to Parliament, enshrined in the Constitution, representing the undeniable will of the Australian people, would change that equation for generations to come.

Importantly, though, we should always see constitutional recognition and the Voice as part of a trilogy – Voice, Treaty, Truth.

ooooo

I came to journalism at the age of twenty, appallingly ignorant of the true history of the country of my birth. The vast majority of the non-Indigenous Australians of my generation and the generations before me had this same ignorance. The existence of the First Nations people barely rated a mention in my formal education. At school I was never given any insights into their rich and enduring civilisation; nor did I learn that these people had been so cruelly and ruthlessly subjugated through the first century and more of white colonial rule. Attending a Christian Brothers school of 1000 children, from 1954 to 1962, I cannot remember a single Indigenous student in any of my classes.

Not only did our national Constitution, introduced in 1901, wash its hands of any responsibility to or for First Nations people who had preceded our 'founding fathers' by at least 60 millennia, it decreed that they should not be counted in the Australian population. No explanation. No justification. Just that bald decree: 'In reckoning the numbers of the people of the Commonwealth, or of a state or other part of the Commonwealth, Aboriginal natives shall not be counted.' As far as the census was concerned Indigenous Australians did not exist.

My personal education about the true history of Australia began with the 1967 referendum to change that part of the Constitution. I had no idea such an exclusion existed. The big historical questions behind the '67 referendum were still not real to me until I went to Alice Springs three years later on an unrelated story. I was shocked to my core by what I saw and what I began to learn about deeply rooted, institutionalised racism. These revelations went against everything I'd been taught growing up as a Catholic kid about the most basic concepts of fairness, about treating others the way we'd like to be treated ourselves.

In 1975 I went back to Alice as a young *Four Corners* journalist to report on that institutionalised racism within the justice system. Specifically, the program was about six young Aboriginal men who'd been framed by concocted confessions for the brutal bashing murder of a young Aboriginal woman. They went to jail pending trial while the most obvious suspect, the murder victim's white de facto partner, disappeared. The charges were eventually thrown out but only because a young, altruistic lawyer named Geoff Eames, later to become a distinguished judge, was running a fledgling Aboriginal legal service there and took up their fight, along with a Uniting Church minister named Jim Downing. Downing could speak the young men's language and was able to comprehensively demonstrate that the police record of their alleged confessions was corrupted and implausible.

The abiding image I took with me as I flew out of Alice Springs in 1975 was of the murder victim's last resting place, a crude, makeshift cross driven into a mound of red dirt on a pauper's grave. And I remember it still when I follow the latest Royal Commission or coronial hearing reflecting the undeniable racism that continues to be deeply imbedded in Australia's various justice systems almost 50 years later, or when I read about yet another Indigenous death in custody.

That is why I find these words in the Uluṟu Statement so particularly heart-wrenching:

> *Proportionally, we are the most incarcerated people on the planet. We are not an innately criminal people. Our children are aliened from their*

families at unprecedented rates. This cannot be because we have no love for them. And our youth languish in detention in obscene numbers. They should be our hope for the future.

These dimensions of our crisis tell plainly the structural nature of our problem. This is the torment of our powerlessness.

∞∞∞

There is another, extremely hopeful side to this critical but unfinished national narrative. Just one year after the *Four Corners* story, a Kuku Yalanji woman from North Queensland named Pat O'Shane became the first Indigenous person to graduate in law in Australia. It made news at the time because, shamefully, it was such an unlikely occurrence. Today, such graduations are no longer regarded as newsworthy because so many Indigenous people are graduating across many academic disciplines around the country.

That progress is reflected in the stream of young, dynamic, articulate Indigenous leaders who are making a significant impact on the mainstream debate. They are contributing in substantial ways in so many fields and so many communities, through the law, through medicine, the arts and academia, through commerce, public administration and the parliaments.

The hope is also nourished by the many young non-Indigenous Australians who are starting their adult life with a much more complete understanding of the true history of their nation. Through what they have learned in school and at university, they recognise the potential for a rich spiritual and material dividend from genuinely shared cultures and values. The best antidote to prejudice is education.

For all that, the sad truth remains, that for every Indigenous person who breaks the cycle of deprivation and injustice there are too many who experience inequity and intergenerational trauma every day. And despite the trail blazed by Pat O'Shane and others, the over-representation of Indigenous peoples in the justice system remains shamefully high, including children as young as ten still being put behind bars.

It was a further eye-opener to me relatively late in life, to learn a reasonably complete story of my own ancestors, the first of whom came from England to the Sydney colony in chains in the 1790s. Others arrived later as refugees from the Irish famine. I could then see with much greater clarity how all the privilege I have enjoyed in my life has sprung initially from family land taken from its Traditional Owners, for which there has never been a proper reckoning.

My ancestors were pioneers, helping to blaze the trail of a new nation, but the land was stolen by white colonial governments and the birthright of Indigenous peoples with it.

Noel Pearson nails it when he reflects on the epic scale of what this country's story will represent when we are genuinely able to come together and acknowledge three intermingled narratives: 'The ancient Indigenous heritage which is its foundation, the British institutions built upon it, and the adorning gift of multicultural migration.'[2] Three strands, one people.

There are many ingrained wrongs still to be put right, many gaps of inequality still to be closed, and the intergenerational wounds run too deep to be healed overnight. Across the decades I have heard many enlightened, knowledgeable people offer their insights into these issues. They have explained why so many expensive, often well-intentioned policies to address the social and economic inequities directly affecting far too many Indigenous people have failed. It is because they are often conceived and executed from the centre of government and rubber-stamped by parliaments far away from the communities they're supposed to be helping. Thanks to these insights, I understand why the Voice to Parliament is so important.

Having also seen many attempts to facilitate Indigenous input to policy processes not properly supported by government, or in the case of ATSIC (Aboriginal and Torres Strait Islander Commission), where the structure was flawed but not given a chance to reform, I also understand why it is important to enshrine a Voice to Parliament in the Constitution. It doesn't eliminate the risk of indifference from the government of the day but it certainly reduces it. And as a permanent institution, it would be guaranteed to have time to mature and evolve, just like the Parliament itself has done.

As a journalist who has borne witness to Australia's ups and downs over the past half-century and often sought to read its moods, I believe there is now a strong collective desire for meaningful reconciliation. I personally experienced the roots of that desire in the Walk for Reconciliation across the Sydney Harbour Bridge on 28 May 2000. It reflected a huge communal wellspring of goodwill – some 250,000 people – the likes of which I have never witnessed before or since. In the absence of inspired political leadership on this issue at the time, we just didn't know where to go from there.

Now the Uluṟu Statement from the Heart is showing us the way. We just need the leadership and the political goodwill to guide the process, not only from Canberra but from every state and region across the land, every municipality, every electorate. Already, every state premier and territory chief minister from both sides of politics has signed on to a statement supporting the referendum to enshrine the Voice in the Constitution.[3]

The public support for the Uluṟu Statement is clearly evident, but not everyone understands the principles behind a Voice to Parliament, why it needs to be in the Constitution and how it might work. That is why I didn't hesitate to take up the invitation from Uluṟu Statement signatory Thomas Mayo to write this short, explanatory book with him on how the Voice might function, on why it would not subvert the parliamentary process in any way, but enhance and strengthen its integrity and, in the process, help make us whole as a nation.

We, the Australian people, can't allow this referendum to descend into the destructive, polarised, partisan politics that has made us all so weary and disillusioned in recent times. And it is a fact of Australian history that 82 per cent of referendums have failed. If we don't all understand what this referendum is for and why, and its opponents are able sufficiently to muddy the waters, it will fail.

If this book works for you, spread it around. Give it to family and friends, colleagues and acquaintances. This is an enormous and long-overdue opportunity presented through the gift of the Uluru Statement for the grassroots of this country to speak up and deliver the result we all need. There is no stronger expression of the public will than for the people of Australia to speak through a referendum, no clearer or more powerful demand for constitutional recognition of First Nations people and the imperative for their voice to be heard.

CHAPTER 1

Introducing the Voice to Parliament

KERRY O'BRIEN AND THOMAS MAYO

There is no mystery about the concept of an Indigenous Voice to Parliament. It has come in many forms over many decades, from voices of angry protest and bark petitions to voices formally invited into the corridors of power to make policy representations.

Until the 1967 referendum, when over 90 per cent of Australians voted resoundingly to give the national Parliament the power to make laws affecting all Indigenous peoples, they had to create their own Voice. It was never easy because most federal politicians before the 1960s tended to echo the sentiments of the states that Indigenous peoples should be assimilated into white society. With few exceptions they were simply not interested in what First Nations people had to say about their own welfare.

That changed to a degree after 1967, when successive federal governments could no longer ignore their responsibility for Indigenous peoples across every nook and cranny of the nation. Gradually they came to accept a formal role for Indigenous voices to help shape policies affecting Indigenous peoples; hardly a radical concept and yet far too often those voices have been ignored.

With practically every government since 1967, but particularly when the government has changed from one side of politics to the other, the means by which Indigenous voices have been heard has changed with it. Sometimes governments have sought to strengthen the Indigenous Voice, sometimes they have weakened or even abolished it. The weaker the formal Voice to Parliament, the easier it is to ignore.

One of the tragedies in all this is that over the decades many billions of dollars have been wasted on poorly informed policies. They have been designed and implemented by non-Indigenous politicians and bureaucrats in Canberra or the state capitals, with little or no input from the very people they are supposed to be helping, many of them living thousands of kilometres away, often in remote communities.

On the principle that Indigenous peoples are best served when they are able to speak for themselves about their own conditions, Australia is a signatory to the UN Declaration on the Rights of Indigenous Peoples, which includes a commitment to self-determination. The Voice, through its grassroots representations, would help to facilitate this often dishonoured commitment.

In a nutshell, there has been no effective continuity or consistency of Indigenous representations from decade to decade, from government to government. Indigenous peoples themselves have rarely had the chance to come together, to learn from the Parliament's mistakes and their own, to build a better, more effective Voice as they go. The 2017 Indigenous consensus supporting the Uluru Statement from the Heart was one such rare opportunity. Indigenous peoples did not waste it.

The Uluru Statement asks for an Indigenous Voice to be enshrined in the Constitution by referendum. If the majority of Australians in a majority of states vote 'Yes' in this referendum, they will provide the moral and political force Indigenous peoples need to finally be heard; they will have created a necessarily compelling Voice that will work with the Executive Government and the Parliament to close the gap.

Constitutional change to guarantee an Aboriginal and Torres Strait Islander Voice will ensure it cannot be silenced or ignored as Indigenous voices have been in the past. Yet, just like any other legislated government agency, the model of the Voice would be decided by elected politicians through the Parliament. Legislation would add the necessary flexibility around the structure of the Voice, supported by the constitutional permanence of the principle to recognise and listen to Indigenous peoples.

There has already been a great deal of detail written about the number of Indigenous representatives who might make up the Voice and how they would be elected to represent Indigenous peoples in each state and territory. The Morrison government, in which the current Opposition Leader Peter Dutton was a senior minister, commissioned a report from an expert group co-chaired by two highly respected Indigenous leaders, Professor Marcia Langton AO and Dr Tom Calma AO, to propose a model for an advisory Voice to Parliament.

Their 280-page report included a proposed model consisting of 24 members, comprising two from each state, territory and the Torres Strait Islands, a further five from remote areas in the Northern Territory, Western Australia, Queensland, New South Wales and South Australia and one Torres Strait Islander living on the mainland. Mr Dutton should be very familiar with that report.

It's neither a difficult nor radical proposition, but whether the final model proposed to the Parliament by the Albanese government post-referendum has 24 members or 30 or 40, it would have to run the gauntlet of parliamentary debate in both the House of Representatives and the Senate before it was decided by vote in both houses.

Once in place, the Voice itself would be judged in the public arena on the quality of its representations, on whether it is faithfully reflecting the collective wisdom of the communities it is representing, and on outcomes. Importantly, the Voice would be accountable to its constituents as well as to the Parliament. On the other hand, Executive Government and the Parliament would be judged on the integrity of their responses.

The people most affected by the policies and laws passed by Parliament would choose who will give advice on their behalf. Not the politicians.

ooooo

Success at this referendum should make a radical difference for the better in the lives of the people who need it most. It is a life-or-death situation for many Indigenous people, so all Australians should be properly informed before they vote.

Some people have sought to complicate this referendum, when really it is quite simple.

Its sole purpose is to decide whether to write into our national rule book – the Constitution – that because of their occupation of the continent as a continuous civilisation for over 60,000 years, and because of the deep injustice of their colonial dispossession, Indigenous peoples have a right to be heard through a Voice to the national Parliament.

It comes down to a question about fairness and acceptance.

For Australians who today more than ever are embracing Indigenous art, languages, dancing and storytelling, and sharing the international kudos accorded to Indigenous cultures, there really is everything to gain and nothing to lose by voting 'Yes'.

∞∞∞∞

We have written this handbook to give the reasons why to vote 'Yes' at the referendum.

In the following chapters, we provide you with truth and information to help you to make your decision. Our aim is that this book will become a useful tool when you're considering how you will vote and in your discussions with family, friends and colleagues.

We have purposely kept it short and chosen a small format that's cheap and easy to post, so you can read it quickly and send copies to anyone you know who might want to find out more about the referendum.

If you decide to vote 'Yes', then we need your help in the weeks and days leading up to the referendum. Talk to others about why you believe an Aboriginal and Torres Strait Islander Voice is important. Having this discussion with even just one or two people could lead to more 'Yes' votes.

Here's one final point to consider, before you read the rest of this book. While some media reports suggest otherwise, research by the CT Group has shown that a clear majority of Indigenous peoples support constitutional recognition because they are compelled by a belief that a successful referendum will be a unifying moment.

The hand is outstretched – we need only to reach out and accept it.

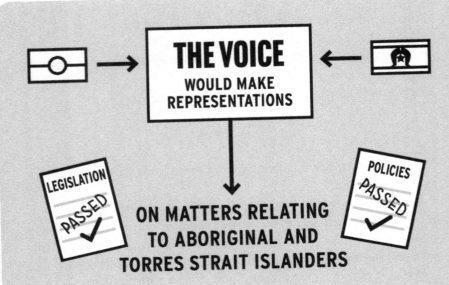

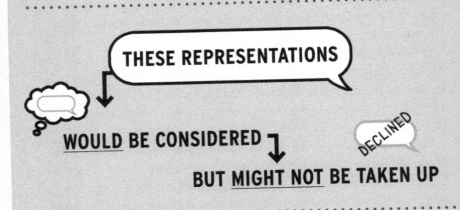

CHAPTER 2

The history of struggle for an effective Voice

KERRY O'BRIEN

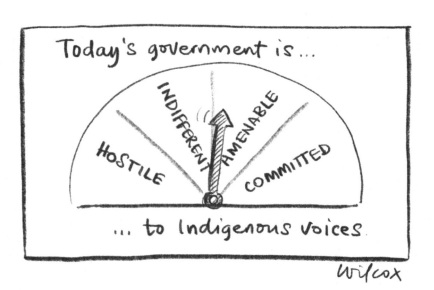

Aboriginal and Torres Strait Islander peoples have every right to feel deeply sceptical about promises to give them, as the first inhabitants of this country, a formal capacity to have a say on matters that directly affect them. There are too many examples of when they have been sidelined by governments in the past.

They had no say in writing Australia's Constitution and indeed were written out of it. In the decades leading up to Federation, the various colonies increasingly regarded Indigenous peoples as a dying race, unable to cope with white civilisation, from which they were mostly excluded anyway.

By the time nationhood was declared in 1901, Indigenous armed resistance across the continent and in Tasmania dating from the earliest days of colonial settlement had been overwhelmed. Many tens of thousands of Indigenous people died in battle or through massacres. In Queensland, the government effectively sanctioned the wholesale killing of Indigenous peoples through the second half of the nineteenth century, where the slaughter was euphemistically described in police reports as 'dispersals'.[1] Often the thinking behind herding Indigenous peoples onto reserves around Australia under 'protective' legislation and into missions was to 'smooth the dying man's pillow'[2] – in other words, to give some semblance of protection to Indigenous peoples while waiting for them to die out.

The history is full of contradictions. While some politicians and bureaucrats subscribed to the theory that Indigenous extinction was inevitable, others feared that numbers would grow big enough to threaten what they believed was the 'orderly and righteous progress of white Australia'. One of Australia's most influential assimilationists in the early decades of nationhood was the Western Australian Chief Protector of Aborigines, AO Neville, who asked a Canberra meeting of his counterparts from around the country in 1937: 'Are we going to have a population of one million blacks in the Commonwealth or are we going to merge them into our white community and eventually forget that there were ever any Aborigines in Australia?'[3]

Neville firmly subscribed to the theory that if 'half-castes', 'quadroons', and 'octeroons' were removed from Indigenous communities and assimilated into white society, the effect would be to 'breed out the colour'.

To one degree or another, the other states and the Northern Territory supported Neville's theories. Another quote, this time from the Northern Territory Administrator in a 1933 report, is shocking to read today: 'Every endeavour is being made to breed out the colour by elevating female half-castes to the white standard with a view to their absorption by mating into the white population.'[4]

Although the Commonwealth Government had no authority over Indigenous affairs in the six states at that time, it sat at the 1937 conference table representing the Aboriginal populations in the Northern Territory and the ACT, and was an enthusiastic supporter of Neville's opinions. Neville's counterpart in Queensland from 1911 to 1940, John Bleakley, at one point defended the need for missions and reserves to act as buffer zones, protecting Indigenous peoples from white predators: 'Not only do they protect the child races from the unscrupulous white, but they help to preserve the purity of the white race from the grave social dangers that always threaten where there is a degraded race living in loose conditions at its back door.'[5]

Among his wide-ranging powers over Indigenous peoples in Queensland, Bleakley could approve the employment of Indigenous girls as young as twelve as domestic servants.[6]

Imagine for a moment the impact of often-expressed attitudes such as these, felt by generations of Indigenous people everywhere.

It was common in the states for police to act as the Chief Protector's agents from region to region, community to community. Fundamentally, official racist policies were backed by force.

∞∞∞

Indigenous peoples had no voice in the policies that would determine their fate and set their course for generations. This included the policies that drove the removal of many thousands of children from their families until the 1970s, particularly Indigenous children who might have a non-Indigenous or, more particularly, a white parent.

The brutal saga of the Stolen Generations is easily accessible to anyone today. Just do an internet search for the Human Rights Commission's *Bringing Them Home* Report. There are reasonably short chapters in the report tracing the history of child removals for each state and the Northern Territory, revealing the policies that produced so much human misery and destruction, driving a stake into the hearts of Indigenous families and communities. It is the personal stories that really enfold you in the truths of a great national tragedy that is still playing out through intergenerational trauma.

It would take just a few minutes to read the chapter about your state or territory. It is a story of institutionalised racism, the cost of which can still be measured in the annual Commonwealth *Closing the Gap* reports, which reveal the ongoing gaps between Indigenous and non-Indigenous Australians across the spectrum of social wellbeing and equality.

∞∞∞

First Nations people have not meekly accepted their exclusion from the power structures and policy-making processes of postcolonial Australia. There has been a long history of activism. But finding and sustaining a voice at the table has always been an uphill battle, because how that voice would be structured and the extent to which it would be heard was always up to white politicians and white bureaucrats to decide. And when there have been breakthroughs from a more enlightened government, in too many cases, incoming governments have either changed or neutered the voice, or simply axed it.

Having said that, the sustained efforts by First Nations people through the decades since Federation, against often powerfully entrenched resistance, building a depth of activism and leadership expertise, have slowly but inexorably pulled the nation through milestones such as the 1967 referendum, land rights legislation, the

Anti-Discrimination Act, ATSIC, the *Mabo* case and now the Uluṟu Statement from the Heart.

In 1924, a Worimi activist named Fred Maynard, founded the Australian Aboriginal Progressive Association (AAPA) to advocate for citizenship, land rights and other fundamental rights related to health, education, employment, housing and child protection. It established thirteen branches with 600 members across New South Wales. In the early days of the Great Depression, it was derailed amidst allegations of strong resistance from the NSW Aboriginal Protection Board and the police. The NSW Chief Police Commissioner at the time was also Chairman of the NSW Aborigines [sic] Protection Board.[7]

The AAPA agitated for the dismantling of the Protection Board after the Board had presided over the closure of independent reserves. From the 1860s, some Indigenous communities had gained access to some of their land for hunting, farming and food gathering. When the land from the reserves was re-allocated to white farmers, it became known as the second dispossession.

A 1983 documentary film called *Lousy Little Sixpence*[8] uses historic footage and interviews with Indigenous activists from the AAPA era to shed light on just how First Nations people were treated through the first half of the twentieth century. The film's title refers to the amount of 'pocket money' the government was supposed to give indentured Aboriginal workers who were forced into servitude. These paltry wages were 'managed' by their employers on behalf of the Aboriginal Protection Board.

Another activists from those years, Yorta Yorta man, William Cooper, was one of the founders of the Australian Aborigines' League (AAL) in 1936. It was formed to lobby state and federal governments on Indigenous rights. Cooper travelled from reserve to reserve collecting 2000 Indigenous signatures on a petition to King George VI calling for First Nations people's representation in the Federal Parliament.

On 26 January 1938, the 150th anniversary of the First Fleet's arrival in Australia, the League called for a National Day of

Mourning to mark the decimation of the Indigenous population over that time. The protestors rallied for 'a new policy which will raise our people to full citizenship status and equality within the community'.[9] A few days later, a delegation including AAL leaders met with Prime Minister Joe Lyons to call for federal control of Indigenous affairs. Their appeal fell on deaf ears.

One month later, the Lyons government formally refused to send Cooper's petition to the King. It was to be another 29 years before an Australian government would act on continuing calls for First Nations people to be formally acknowledged in the national census and for Federal Parliament to acknowledge its national responsibility for Indigenous affairs.

William Cooper's nephew, Pastor Doug Nicholls (later Sir Douglas, the first Indigenous Australian to be knighted) took up the cudgel through the Federal Council for the Advancement of Aborigines and Torres Strait Islanders (FCAATSI), established in 1958 with the great North Queensland activist Faith Bandler and others.

Nicholls was a gifted AFL footballer who played for Fitzroy in the 1930s, becoming the first Indigenous player to be selected to play for the Victorian interstate team. In his first year at Fitzroy, Nicholls was forced to use a separate change room from his teammates and suffered racist taunts on the field.

Sir Doug's experiences in the 1930s are emblematic of the broader national narrative of Australia's long up and down struggle to come to grips with its endemic history of racism, reconcile its Indigenous and non-Indigenous peoples and embrace a common future. He had to confront racism on the field and in the grandstand.

Sixty years later, AFL greats Nicky Winmar and Michael Long were still fighting very public battles against racism in 1993 and 1995. Winmar famously called it out at the end of a heated, take-no-prisoners St Kilda game against Collingwood after copping sustained racial abuse. He lifted his jersey, pointed to his skin and declared, 'I'm black and I'm proud to be black.' Collingwood president, Allan McAlister, said on television that Collingwood had no issue with Indigenous people, 'As long as they conducted themselves like white people, well, off the field everyone will admire and respect them.'[10]

Michael Long's stand two years later forced the AFL to adopt a racial abuse code and umpires were instructed to report racist incidents. Yet twenty years later again, Adam Goodes, a highly respected dual Brownlow medalist, was booed out of the game for once again calling out racial abuse. It's the same story in our political history – the slow, painful dance of two steps forward and one step back with no policy advance set in stone.

Nicholls, Bandler and other leaders in the Federal Council for the Advancement of Aborigines and Torres Strait Islanders, drove a new petition proposing constitutional change to allow the Commonwealth to make laws on behalf of First Nations people – this time collecting more than 100,000 signatures by 1962. One year later, the Yolŋu people of Arnhem Land presented two further petitions on bark to the national Parliament, protesting the lack of consultation with them over the establishment of a bauxite mine on their Country and the impact it would have. Territories Minister Paul Hasluck rejected the first petition, challenging the validity of signatures. The second bark petition added the thumbprints of clan Elders.

The 1962 and 1963 petitions failed in their immediate intent, but both undoubtedly added to the pressure building on the Holt government to introduce the 1967 referendum.

Faith Bandler stands out as an inspirational figure in her decade-long campaign for a referendum. Her father had been kidnapped as a boy from the New Hebrides, now Vanuatu, in 1883, to work on sugar plantations in North Queensland. The hardest part of the campaign for a referendum, she said, was 'to get people to think of the Aboriginal people as people'.[11] Yet the 1967 referendum remains the most resounding 'Yes' vote in 122 years.

After that 'Yes' vote, the Holt government's response to its newfound powers to make laws to tackle the ingrained inequality of Indigenous peoples was underwhelming at best. Two months later, in July 1967, the Federal Minister for Territories, Charles Barnes, was 'unable to give any indication as to how the Commonwealth might use its new powers'.[12]

The Prime Minister Harold Holt, however, was interested enough to create a three-person Council for Aboriginal Affairs (CAA) attached to his new Office of Aboriginal Affairs (OAA) in November 1967. The CAA was to be chaired by Dr HC Coombs, a career public servant and first governor of the Reserve Bank, with a career diplomat, Barrie Dexter, and the eminent anthropologist, Bill Stanner, as his co-councillors – all white men. Only Stanner had any real knowledge of Indigenous history and culture.

As administrative head of the office, Dexter recruited two former government patrol officers 'on the basis of their knowledge of Aboriginal peoples'.[13] One was a former Northern Territory Director of Native Welfare, Frank Moy, who had played a leading role in suppressing a 1950–51 strike by Aboriginal workers in Darwin over poor wages and living conditions in a compound outside the city.

When another strike leader, Larrakia man Frank Waters, organised a lightning strike, Frank Moy used his administrative power to banish Waters to Haasts Bluff mission, 1700 kilometres away in Central Australia.

Harold Holt drowned in December 1967, when his Council of Aboriginal Affairs was still being set up, but his successor, John Gorton, went further, establishing Australia's first Department of Aboriginal Affairs, with a junior minister, William Wentworth. Gorton was still an assimilationist who opposed the growing support for Indigenous land rights.[14]

Barrie Dexter, who went on to run the Department of Aboriginal Affairs under Gough Whitlam, wrote of Gorton in a book, *Pandora's Box*, many years later that: 'No doubt the prime minister's lack of interest and sympathy reflected itself in the non-cooperative, unfriendly and even hostile attitude of his department towards the OAA [Office of Aboriginal Affairs] and the council.'[15]

Coombs was also damning of Gorton's lack of commitment, writing fifteen years later: 'Unfortunately Gorton's image of Australian society, like that of many of his compatriots, had no place for Aborigines as such. He saw no justification or need for special policies to help them and the idea that Aborigines had valid rights to land based on traditional title was to him wholly unacceptable.'[16]

After three tumultuous years, Billy McMahon deposed Gorton as Prime Minister, and the situation became even more farcical. When McMahon named another enthusiastic assimilationist, Peter Howson, as his new Minister for the Environment, Aborigines (sic) and the Arts, an ungrateful Howson reportedly snarled to a colleague that 'The little bastard [McMahon] gave me trees, boongs and poofters.'[17]

Perhaps the biggest aggravation by Indigenous activists in the McMahon era was the establishment of the Aboriginal Tent Embassy on 26 January 1972 in front of what is now Old Parliament House, as a protest over Billy McMahon's rejection of land rights. Fifty-one years later, it's still there and must stand as one of the most effective and enduring forms of protest in our modern history.

Gough Whitlam's commitment to First Nations people stood in stark contrast to McMahon's marked disinterest. Whitlam declared in his campaign launch for the 1972 election: 'We will legislate to give Aborigines [sic] land rights – not just because their case is beyond argument, but because all of us as Australians are diminished while the Aborigines are denied their rightful place in this nation.'

One of his first actions after being voted into office on 2 December, even before his government had been formed, was to set his promised Royal Commission into land rights in train. Within three months of the election the process had begun to establish Australia's first elected Indigenous Voice to a national government – the National Aboriginal Consultative Committee (NACC) – to 'restore to Aboriginals the power to make their own decisions about their way of life'.[18] The committee had 41 elected Indigenous delegates from around Australia, who would give advice to their minister on behalf of all Indigenous peoples.

Aboriginal Land Councils were established and money began to flow into Indigenous health, housing, legal aid, education and employment. But regardless of the quality of advice from the NACC, social policies were still heavily influenced and administered by the central bureaucratic control in Canberra. The result was a patchwork of success and failure. At least land rights were delivered to the Northern Territory as an example for the states to follow when the Federal Parliament passed the *Aboriginal Land Rights (Northern Territory) Act* in December 1976.

After the Whitlam government's dismissal in 1975, it was left to the new Prime Minister, Malcolm Fraser, to do the right thing and support Whitlam's land rights legislation through the Parliament. Fraser also accepted Whitlam's commitment to having an Indigenous advisory Voice to government, although he did replace the National Aboriginal Consultative Committee with another body called the National Aboriginal Conference (NAC), with 35 full-time salaried members, state and territory branches and a more restrictive voting system.

Both fledgling organisations were destabilised by tensions with the Department of Aboriginal Affairs, and at times with the minister. Under Fraser, national Indigenous policy continued to be dominated and driven from Canberra – remote from most of the communities the government sought to serve. Those who opposed the whole idea of First Nations people actually participating in the government and policy process were always quick to capitalise on the failures. Occasional calls for a treaty or for self-determination didn't really go anywhere.

Like the NACC before it, the NAC was axed in 1985, two years into the Hawke government. One year later, Bob Hawke walked away from a firm promise to introduce national land rights legislation that would force the states to follow the example set by Whitlam in the Northern Territory. The national land rights bill was to have held Aboriginal land under inalienable freehold title, protected sacred sites and decreed Aboriginal control in relation to mining on Aboriginal land. It was dumped by Hawke under heavy pressure from the mining industry and the Burke Labor government in Western Australia.

Hawke promised in 1988, in response to a petition from the Central and Northern Land Councils known as the Barunga Statement, that his government would facilitate a treaty to achieve a lasting reconciliation. That promise was dishonoured too, as reflected in the Yothu Yindi anthem 'Treaty', whose words perfectly underscore the argument for having a Voice to Parliament enshrined in the Constitution.

The closest Hawke came to honouring his promise was to establish a Council for Aboriginal Reconciliation in 1991, but he was replaced as Prime Minister by Paul Keating at the end of that year. The council laboured on with a brief to 'raise awareness' and produce 'a document of reconciliation' within a decade. Concrete outcomes are hard to measure, other than the symbolically powerful People's Walk for Reconciliation, where around 250,000 people crossed the Sydney Harbour Bridge in May 2000.

Keating described Hawke's surrender on land rights as 'one of the rare moral low points of the Hawke government'.[19] On the other hand, in 1989 Hawke did preside over an Act of Parliament that created the Aboriginal and Torres Strait Islander Commission (ATSIC), which was to give First Nations people by far their most powerful voice to government and the Parliament up to that point.

After twenty years of trial and error post-1967, with most of Australia still woefully ignorant of its oldest culture, ATSIC arrived with a great deal of hope that a national government was finally ready to embrace a partnership with a genuinely representative Aboriginal and Torres Strait Island Voice.

ATSIC was based on 35 regional councils around Australia, to be elected every three years, supported by a well-resourced administrative arm. Its brief was to develop its own policies, while still answerable to the Minister for Aboriginal Affairs, Gerry Hand. The councils were grouped into sixteen zones, including for the first time the Torres Strait Islands, and each zone selected one representative to serve on a national board of commissioners, with the chair initially appointed by the minister.

Suffice to say that ATSIC chalked up achievements and failures. With no precedent for such an ambitious attempt to provide Indigenous Australia with an effective and influential voice at the national table, genuinely reflecting the views and needs of communities and individuals around the nation, of course there were going to be mistakes. Indigenous politics are no different to any other brand in a democracy in the sense that the path to policy compromise was accompanied by all the normal tensions between grassroots Indigenous expectations and their elected representatives, between the regional councils and their sixteen commissioners, and between the commission and its minister as well as his bureaucrats.

While ATSIC was still establishing itself, with a remarkable Pitjantjatjara woman Lowitja O'Donoghue as its first chair, the High Court handed down its historic judgement in the *Mabo* case in June 1992. The judgement ended the offensive 200-year concept of *terra nullius* on which white Australia had been built, that the continent was nobody's land, thereby justifying the systematic dispossession of Indigenous peoples. The *Mabo* case superseded all previous High Court decisions, which had held that Native Title rights to Traditional lands had been extinguished since white settlement.

Paul Keating, in his first year as Prime Minister, took up the challenge posed by the *Mabo* ruling. As various powerful voices of dissent from *Mabo* emerged, particularly pastoralists, the mining industry and state governments wanting to control their own patch, Keating signalled his intent with the now famous Redfern Park Speech of December 1992. In it he said that the *Mabo* case established a fundamental truth and laid the basis for justice:

The starting point might be to recognise that the problem starts with us non-Aboriginal Australians. It begins, I think, with that of recognition. Recognition that it was we who did the dispossessing. We took the traditional lands and smashed the traditional way of life. We brought the diseases. The alcohol. We committed the murders. We took the children from their mothers. We practiced discrimination and exclusion.

It was our ignorance and our prejudice. And our failure to imagine these things being done to us.

Mabo represented the first time in Australia's postcolonial history that Aboriginal and Torres Strait Island leaders sat as equals at the negotiating table with all the other vested interests, to thrash out a practical but principled formula for Native Title to make sense of the

High Court ruling. Ultimately the legislation was a classic compromise, but it didn't sell Indigenous Traditional Owners down the river.

Those negotiations through 1993 demonstrated the depth and quality of Indigenous leadership that had by now emerged around the nation. Up until this point people in that role had always been hampered in formal negotiations by their reluctance to speak with any authority beyond their own clan or nation, because no one leader could speak for all Indigenous peoples. Keating's attempt to negotiate an outcome to *Mabo* could never have succeeded unless that tradition changed.

At this time, Lowitja O'Donoghue stepped up. As the Foundation Chair of ATSIC from 1990 to 1996, she had a platform to speak from, but no power or authority beyond that prescribed role. With the sheer force of her will and sense of moral authority, O'Donoghue forged a leadership team to negotiate with the Commonwealth. It was drawn from the Indigenous Land Councils, whose own battle-hardened skills had been shaped through long years of negotiation with big mining companies and state and territory governments.

Sitting around the Cabinet table with Keating and other government negotiators, at the epicentre of Australian democracy, O'Donoghue's group ultimately included David Ross from the Central Land Council, Daryl Pearce from the Northern Land Council, Peter Yu from the Kimberley Land Council, Noel Pearson, a dynamic new voice from the Cape York Land Council, Getano Lui from the Torres Strait Islands Coordinating Council, Rob Reilly from the Legal Service of Western Australia, Mick Dodson, the Social Justice Commissioner, and Pat Dodson, the chair of the Council for Aboriginal Reconciliation. Professor Marcia Langton was an adviser.

The result was the *Native Title Act 1993*, which reflected compromise by all parties but provided a pathway for orderly processing of Indigenous claims to Native Title around Australia. It was supported by a social justice package, including a land fund – with funding locked in for a decade, to support Indigenous peoples who had been victims of dispossession through colonial settlement but who were unable to prove Native Title rights – to purchase land.

Noel Pearson subsequently wrote that: 'Never before and likely never again would Indigenes be invited in from the woodheap to sit at the main table as they did during those Keating years.'[20] As one of the authors of the Uluru Statement in 2017, Pearson will be happy for the people of Australia to prove him wrong on that score at least, when they vote in the Voice referendum.

When John Howard replaced Paul Keating as Prime Minister in March 1996, the writing was on the wall for ATSIC and for Native Title. Howard as Opposition Leader had opposed ATSIC because 'it strikes at the heart of the unity of the Australian people'.[21] He said the Coalition would never support a treaty and had voted against the Native Title legislation in 1993. He wrote in his autobiography in 2010 that he had not been 'all that sympathetic' to the *Bringing Them Home* inquiry on the Stolen Generations set up by Keating in 1995, and had refused to commit to its future funding. He also complained that 'virtually all of the Aboriginal leadership shared the Labor view of Indigenous affairs'.[22]

In December 1996, a further ruling by the High Court involving a Native Title claim over two pastoral leases by the Wik People in the North Queensland Gulf Country, that Native Title rights could coexist on land held by pastoral leases, gave the Howard government cause to revisit Keating's Native Title Act.

John Howard dismissed the existing laws as 'nothing more than an administrative nightmare' and his Deputy Prime Minister, Tim Fischer, called for 'bucketloads of extinguishment'.[23] Respected Indigenous leader Professor Marcia Langton described the storm over *Wik* as 'manufactured hysteria', pointing out that pastoralists' security of tenure in Australia was not in jeopardy. But Howard significantly watered down the laws, making it more difficult for Indigenous claimants to successfully pursue their Native Title claims.

His government also ordered a review on the effectiveness of ATSIC in 2002, after six years of friction over governance and other issues. The review was headed by a former Liberal New South Wales

Attorney-General, John Hannaford, and there was a great deal of speculation that it would lead to the axing of the Commission. Hannaford's report late in 2003 found that rather than being shut down, ATSIC should continue but needed urgent structural change to give greater control to Aboriginal and Torres Strait Islander peoples at a regional level 'to stimulate change where it is most needed'.[24] It was ironic that one of the review's criticisms of ATSIC was that it had become too centralised in Canberra.

Instead of restructuring ATSIC, the Howard government did decide to shut it down in April 2004, supported by Mark Latham as Opposition Leader. The man who had first sponsored ATSIC and oversaw its design in the Hawke years, Gerry Hand, said it was simplistic in the extreme to hold ATSIC responsible for all the problems facing Indigenous peoples and he feared that whatever replaced it would 'also end up being a scapegoat'. Hand said ATSIC failed because the regions grew apart from the centralised structure,[25] which echoed the findings of the ATSIC review that the Howard government commissioned and then effectively ignored.

Another former Aboriginal Affairs Minister under Malcolm Fraser, Fred Chaney, who by 2004 was co-chair of Reconciliation Australia, said ATSIC had clearly become 'a dustbin for every bit of blame there was'.[26] Senator Amanda Vanstone, the Indigenous Affairs Minister at the time ATSIC was abolished, admitted to a Parliamentary Joint Select Committee on Constitutional Recognition in 2018 that in hindsight the complete abolition of ATSIC 'might have been a mistake'. Had there been constitutional recognition of a Voice to Parliament back in 2003, ATSIC could have been changed, even radically, by a combination of government and Parliament, but as an Indigenous Voice to Parliament it could not have been abolished.

In the years since ATSIC, through the next five governments, Labor and Liberal, leading up to the election of the Albanese government in 2022, various structures to provide Indigenous representation to the national government and Parliament have too often been a chequerboard of disappointment.

It has to be acknowledged, however, that although the pathway to the Uluru Statement from the Heart in 2017 was a long and tortuous one in terms of government input, both Labor and Coalition governments did contribute to the final outcome. The Gillard government set up an Expert Panel to facilitate the recognition of Aboriginal and Torres Strait Islander peoples in 2010, which reported two years later, recommending significant constitutional change. In 2015, Prime Minister Malcolm Turnbull and Opposition Leader Bill Shorten together agreed after meeting with Indigenous leaders, to establish a Referendum Council. This, in turn, set up the First Nations Constitutional Dialogues through 2016–17, leading to the First Nations Constitutional Convention at Uluru in 2017, and thus the Uluru Statement from the Heart was born.

The tragedy of that whole saga was that Prime Minister Turnbull so perfunctorily dismissed the Uluru Statement's call for a constitutionally enshrined Voice to Parliament as unacceptable, claiming it could act as a third chamber of Parliament. That view has been discredited. The Parliament has the constitutional power to make or reject laws. The Indigenous Voice to Parliament could not. It could only seek to positively enlighten the policy deliberations of government and the Parliament by making suggestions from outside the Parliament, like so many other advisory bodies in other fields. The one important difference between the Voice and other Indigenous advisory bodies of the past is that the existence of the Voice would be guaranteed by the Constitution.

ooooo

A low point for relations between Canberra and most of Australia's Indigenous leadership was the Howard government's heavy-handed Intervention policy in scores of remote Indigenous communities in the Northern Territory in August 2007. It was framed as a 'national emergency' three months before the election that John Howard lost to Kevin Rudd. The Australian Army was deployed, ostensibly in a logistical and administrative role supporting the Howard government's Intervention to protect Aboriginal children from sexual abuse, but the whole operation was headed by a senior army officer, elevating the military's role and giving the exercise a sense of high drama. The range of measures and the way they were implemented would have been unthinkable in other Australian communities. The broadly felt stigma was appalling.

The *Racial Discrimination Act 1975* (Cth) had to be suspended to prevent the process being illegal. In other words, the Intervention was fundamentally discriminatory. As we all well know, domestic violence and child abuse in Australia are not confined to any one social or ethnic group but are certainly linked to social deprivation and poverty, a cycle that is often reflected from generation to generation. The hard truth is that these issues and their underlying causes across mainstream Australia have often been chronically underfunded until the very recent past, but nowhere else has there been an intervention like that in the Northern Territory. The Intervention was not opposed by the Labor Opposition, and was continued by the Rudd and Gillard governments until 2012. And while Kevin Rudd's apology in Parliament in 2008 to the Stolen Generations' survivors was a powerfully symbolic gesture at the time, the government's commitment to closing the gap in all the headline areas of Indigenous disadvantage has had limited success in the fifteen years since. The issues that led to the Intervention might have been handled much more effectively if Indigenous representations had been available to the Howard government from an advisory group like the Voice.

There was no such Indigenous Voice in 2007.

ooooo

What this catalogue of government action and inaction and of the various milestones of Indigenous advocacy shows is that whether Indigenous policy has been enlightened or not, whether personalities within governments have been genuine in their commitment to Indigenous issues or not, the implementation of policy from government to government has been unstable and inconsistent.

There has been no guarantee that the voices of Indigenous leaders would have access to the corridors of power, let alone effective influence. When gains were made there was no guarantee those gains would be protected into the future.

Part of the driving force behind the Uluru Statement and the call for an Indigenous Voice to Parliament to be enshrined in the Constitution, as a direct and powerful expression of the wishes of the Australian people, is that the moral and political weight behind it will make it extremely difficult for future governments to whittle away the strength of such a Voice. Even though the Voice would be an advisory body only to the government of the day and the Parliament, with no power to veto policy it disagrees with, any future government that did not properly fund, support and give due respect to its representations would be judged accordingly.

With its continuity guaranteed in the Constitution, the Voice would be able to mature and evolve as an effective part of the ongoing drive to close the gap on the inequities built into Australian society over 235 years. It could also make serious inroads on the dysfunction and trauma so starkly reflected in the statistics that conflict dramatically with the image we like to project of ourselves as a nation to the world.

CHAPTER 3

The Voice is about who we are as Australians

KERRY O'BRIEN

The most common model of settler colonialism was well and truly in place around much of the world long before Governor Arthur Phillip set up shop in Sydney Cove in January 1788, together with his shiploads of convicts and soldiers, on behalf of King George III.

The major European colonising powers – Britain, Spain, Portugal, France and the Netherlands – had already established a pattern of conquer, subjugate and exploit through much of Africa, Asia and North and South America. 'Gold, God and Glory' was one common historical euphemism.

The legacy has varied from continent to continent, from civilisation to civilisation, but Indigenous populations have never fared well. White supremacy was at the core. To help justify the various degrees of ruthlessness and brutality the colonisers employed, they depicted the local people as racially inferior. Christian missionaries were often willing partners in this colonising process. Around the world, they went about God's business of converting the so-called 'heathens' to Christianity, the only form of spirituality they would recognise.

Colonisation bred slavery and for the colonisers, life was cheap. For example, in the first 100 years of Spanish rule in Central and South America, from 1520 to 1620, it is estimated that the Aztec and Inca civilisations lost 90 per cent of their populations.[1]

In the new colony of Sydney, 250 years after Cortez invaded Central America, the deadliest attack by the settlers on the Indigenous peoples was not armed conflict but the spread of smallpox. It raged throughout Dyarubbin Country along the Hawkesbury-Nepean River and killed up to 80 per cent of people in the area inside the first two years of Phillip's settlement.[2]

As elsewhere, the British colonisers came to Australia as invaders, arrogantly assuming that by sticking a flag in the ground, they had some magic right to claim ownership of a land they knew nothing about. They did not recognise that for over 60,000 years, hundreds of thousands of people lived on this land within the structures of a civilisation made up of many different territories.

If aliens dropped on Australia from space tomorrow, saw us conveniently as an inferior culture and decided to colonise our country, we would call them invaders. Of course we would, and that is what Governor Phillip did 235 years ago.

The colonial settlers' often violent onslaughts through the first century of settlement and more were widely and thoroughly documented, but most of the records gathered dust in government archives.

It is now undeniable that these attacks were either officially sanctioned or unofficially perpetrated, or both, through warfare and massacres and through exclusion from the justice system.

Rounding out the picture are the bureaucratic and political records that document more recent government attempts to assimilate, if not eradicate, Indigenous peoples. The revelations of the inquiry into the Stolen Generations represent just one source. But the truth has been a long time coming. A great shroud of silence around the least palatable aspects of our colonial history and the denial of Indigenous history, culture and occupation have severely diminished our national narrative. Until relatively recently First Nations people have been rendered largely invisible, without a voice, without a seat at the table.

There is no more striking example of this than the Australian Constitution, which came into law in 1901 after years of deliberation and consultation. Indigenous peoples were denied any involvement in composing the Constitution and were essentially written out of it.

Even Indigenous soldiers who put their lives on the line for their country in the First and Second World Wars still felt the sting of discrimination when they came home.

And when the Australian media began slowly to break the Great Australian Silence in the 1960s, as Indigenous activists increasingly found their voice, they were almost always painted as victims. This did not address their legitimacy or their proud history. Their predicament was never really about helplessness or lack of capacity, but about powerlessness. With that powerlessness came the institutionalised poverty and social deprivation that inevitably led to community breakdown, on which Indigenous peoples were then judged.

The Indigenous fight for a voice in the corridors of power has always been contested by non-Indigenous forces and never fully embraced by the Parliament after Federation. Even when a body such as ATSIC was created by the Hawke government in 1989 as a significant Indigenous Voice to Parliament, it was scrapped by the Howard government with the support of the Latham Labor Opposition, against the advice of the government's own review. Without constitutional protection, an Indigenous Voice has no guarantee of permanence and can be stopped at the whim of any government that can gain majority support in both houses of Parliament.

It is in all our interests to see effective and well-informed policies introduced that address the fundamental problems and attempt to close the gap of inequality for Indigenous peoples across so many social and economic benchmarks.

The idea of a constitutionally validated Voice to Parliament reflects the principle that whatever model is adopted, it should enable genuine dialogue between Indigenous communities and their Voice representatives on policies being considered by the Executive Government and the Parliament that will have an impact on them. That dialogue would then be reflected in their representations. The community representatives within the Voice structure would be judged by their own people as to whether grassroots views were being accurately represented.

If the Parliament were then to give respectful consideration to the Voice recommendations for changes or additions to policy, and the final legislation were to genuinely reflect the best analysis from all perspectives, then surely we would see better outcomes on the ground. This would particularly be the case if local Indigenous peoples were directly engaged in the implementation.

The Voice would have input into many of the problem areas facing First Nations people that have been intractable in the past – health, education, housing and employment, for a start – as Indigenous communities move closer to self-determination.

ooooo

Everyone has a stake in the game.

As a nation we have constantly sought to paint ourselves as the land of the fair go. Somewhere within most of us is the desire to do the right thing. For practically the whole of our postcolonial history, the most glaring barrier to that instinct or any claim to egalitarianism has been what Professor Megan Davis, one of the key architects of the Uluru Statement from the Heart, describes as 'the unfinished business of this nation'.[3]

The referendum offers an opportunity for us all to have a direct say in an outcome that is so clearly in all our interests – enshrining Indigenous recognition and the Voice in the Constitution.

One way to measure what a 'Yes' vote for constitutional recognition would mean to us is to imagine how we would feel, individually and collectively, to wake up on the morning after the referendum and contemplate what we'd just achieved as a nation. It would be a clear and positive statement of intent to our politicians, to all the vested interests, to each other, to the world at large and most of all, to First Nations people from Albany at the bottom of Western Australia to the Torres Strait Islands off the tip of Cape York.

We would wake up one big step closer to being a unified country where we formally recognise that the first peoples to settle Australia have lived here for millennia and are the longest continuous culture in the world. All Australians would share this unique heritage. This would be such a gift for the children of coming generations.

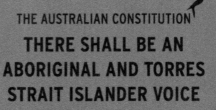

THE AUSTRALIAN CONSTITUTION

THERE SHALL BE AN ABORIGINAL AND TORRES STRAIT ISLANDER VOICE

(SET IN STONE BY REFERENDUM)

ABORIGINAL AND TORRES STRAIT ISLANDER PEOPLES

TOGETHER
↓
DECIDE HOW

THE VOICE WOULD OPERATE

PARLIAMENTARIANS

CHAPTER 4

What is a referendum?

KERRY O'BRIEN AND THOMAS MAYO

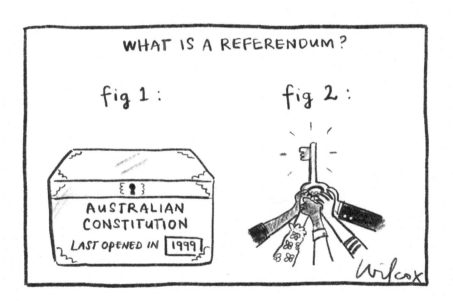

The Australian Constitution defines the powers and structures under which our nation is governed. Even though it came into being as an Act of the British Parliament six months before the Commonwealth of Australia was born on 1 January 1901, the Constitution can only really be changed by a special direct vote of the Australian people.

We can argue until hell freezes over whether the authors of the Constitution should have made it so hard to change the rule book, but hard it is. Various governments over the past 122 years have sought to make 44 changes to the Constitution in nineteen referendums. Some referendums posed a single question for people to vote on and others posed several. Only eight referendum questions out of 44 were successful. That's a success rate of 18 per cent, which is why modern governments don't try very often, and why, when we have the chance to make an important change and the public mood is for it, that we don't want to mess it up.

The reason why referendums are so difficult to pass is that they require not only a majority of voters across the nation voting 'Yes', but also a majority of 'Yes' votes in a majority of states. In other words, more than 50 per cent of voters in four of the six states have to vote 'Yes', as well as the nation as a whole. The votes of citizens in the two territories, the ACT and the Northern Territory, count towards the national tally but the territories are not counted in determining the majority of states.

Because some states have small populations compared to others, say Tasmania compared to New South Wales, if the referendum was simply decided on a national majority of votes, then the bigger states would have much more influence on the result than the smaller states. If the referendum was decided just on how a majority of states voted, then the people of Tasmania would have a much more influential vote than the people of New South Wales. That's what can happen when your country is a federation of states.

The first referendum in 1906 was an obvious commonsense measure to try to align Senate elections with those for the House of Representatives, so people could vote for both chambers of Parliament at the same time. The public voted 'Yes', presumably because it meant they wouldn't have to vote quite so often.

The biggest single 'Yes' vote to change the Constitution was the 1967 referendum introduced by the Holt government to remove the racist provision that excluded Indigenous peoples from being counted in the national census, and to give the Commonwealth Government the power to make laws and introduce policies supposedly for the benefit of Aboriginal people. It was widely supported by both sides of politics. The vote in favour ranged from 81 per cent in Western Australia to 91 per cent in Victoria. Out of 1278 electoral sub-divisions only one registered a negative vote.[1]

On the other hand, the most recent referendum to be introduced was for Australia to become a republic in 1999. It was resoundingly defeated after a very contentious and divisive campaign.

∞∞∞∞

A referendum is not the same as a plebiscite, such as the 2017 plebiscite that asked the Australian people if they would support legislation for marriage equality. The marriage equality plebiscite was unnecessary. The Parliament has the constitutional power to make laws about marriage without asking the Australian people for a mandate between elections.

Constitutional change is different. A change to the laws enshrined in the Constitution can only be made through a successful referendum, which requires two processes, both involving a vote. First, both houses of Parliament have to vote to approve the holding of the referendum and its wording. Second, the proposal for change is then put to the nation for a vote. Voting in a referendum is compulsory for citizens over eighteen, just like an election.

In the 1999 referendum when Australians were asked to vote for or against becoming a republic, they rejected the proposition on both benchmarks. It wasn't even close. The national vote was 54.87 per cent 'No' and 45.13 per cent 'Yes'. All six states voted to reject a republic.

The figures, however, don't tell the whole story. The republican movement was deeply divided between those who wanted a republic with a president elected by the people and those who wanted the Parliament to have the final say on who the president should be.

The Prime Minister at the time, John Howard, was opposed to a republic. He was compelled by public pressure, and pressure from pro-republicans within his own party ranks, to put the proposition to a referendum. However, he virtually guaranteed its defeat by asking Australians to vote for one particular model, knowing that many pro-republicans would vote against it because they wanted a different model.

It would be bizarre to expect a referendum to be successful without the support of the prime minister of the day. And it was clear that Mr Howard did not believe Australia should be a republic. That sentiment, combined with the fact that republicans were divided over whether a president should be elected by the people or by the Parliament, meant the referendum was doomed to fail from the outset.

There is a lesson in this for people who are supporting a referendum on a Voice to Parliament. It is to keep the question being put in the referendum as simple as possible. The more unnecessary complications that are introduced, the more the opponents of the referendum can confuse the picture and the greater the chance that it will fail.

Blatantly false claims have been made already, such as the claim that the Voice would act as a third chamber of Parliament, and that it could veto policy in the Parliament. Indigenous peoples through the Uluru Statement are very clearly not asking for such powers, the Albanese government wouldn't grant them and nor would the Parliament. These claims are designed to scare people into voting 'No'.

If a majority of Australians in a majority of states were to vote for a Voice to Parliament, it would be up to the Parliament – representing all political points of view – to decide how that body would be structured and how it would be funded.

It's neither necessary nor reasonable to try to enshrine the structure of the Voice in the Constitution. If it were to be a third chamber of Parliament, as some politicians have tried to argue, then that detail *would* need to be in the Constitution. But it's not a third chamber and it would be the job of the elected members of Parliament to determine the structure of the Voice as an advisory body situated *outside* the Parliament. That's a debate for MPs to have in the House of Representatives and the Senate and then to pass the laws that would create the Voice. From that point on, the power and influence of the Voice would depend on the wisdom and quality and credibility of its representations to the Executive Government and the Parliament.

The Executive Government and Parliament would be compelled to be seen to give serious consideration to the Voice whenever it is planning to introduce policies that will potentially impact Indigenous communities, but it would not be compelled to adopt that advice – in its entirety or at all. But if the Parliament rejects the advice of the Voice, those who voted against it would have to justify their actions to the public and face public scrutiny for those actions. That is how democracy works.

One of the keys to a successful referendum is to muster as much bipartisanship as possible, and in that regard, the role of the states can't be underestimated. There are some positive signs in this regard. All state premiers and territory chief ministers from both sides of politics have formally supported the referendum. Political support for the referendum at a federal level will be more likely if politicians can see that there is a clear public desire to enshrine Indigenous recognition in the Constitution in this way.

DOUBLE MAJORITY

NATIONAL MAJORITY

AND

YES IN AT LEAST 4 OUT OF
6 STATES

CHAPTER 5

Why vote 'Yes' and other frequently asked questions

THOMAS MAYO AND KERRY O'BRIEN

What is the Voice to Parliament?

The Voice would be a group of Indigenous representatives chosen by Indigenous peoples from around the nation who may make representations to the Executive Government and Parliament on matters that affect them.

What is the proposed referendum question?

A Proposed Law: to alter the Constitution to recognise the First Peoples of Australia by establishing an Aboriginal and Torres Strait Islander Voice. DO YOU APPROVE THIS PROPOSED ALTERATION?

This is the proposed question at the time this book went to print. It might change slightly before the referendum.

Why vote 'Yes'?

A 'Yes' vote would give constitutional recognition to Australia's First Nations people in the form proposed in the Uluru Statement from the Heart – by establishing the principle that Aboriginal and Torres Strait Islander peoples will have a say about the laws and policies that affect their communities through a Voice to Parliament.

This would be a unifying, nation-building act of reconciliation. It would showcase Australia's unique place in the world with over 60,000 years of unbroken heritage and culture.

What would the Voice look like and how would it function?

The proposed alteration to the Constitution establishes the principle that Indigenous peoples should have a say through a Voice.

If the referendum is successful, the elected members of Parliament will then work out the composition, powers, functions and procedures of the Voice with Aboriginal and Torres Strait Islander peoples. The Voice would be based on the following design principles that are drawn from the Langton and Calma Indigenous Voice

Co-design Process and what Indigenous peoples said in the Uluṟu Dialogues. These principles have been finessed by the Referendum Working Group to help Australians understand how the Voice will work (see below).

Design Principles of the Aboriginal and Torres Strait Islander Voice

A Voice to Parliament will be a permanent body to make representations to the Australian Parliament and the Executive Government on legislation and policy of significance to Aboriginal and Torres Strait Islander peoples. It will further the self-determination of Aboriginal and Torres Strait Islander peoples, by giving them a greater say on matters that affect them.

The following are the design principles of the Voice to Parliament agreed by the First Nations Referendum Working Group:

A. The Voice will give independent advice to the Parliament and Government

- The Voice would make representations to the Parliament and the Executive Government on matters relating to Aboriginal and Torres Strait Islander peoples.
- The Voice would be able to make representations proactively.
- The Voice would be able to respond to requests for representations from the Parliament and the Executive Government.
- The Voice would have its own resources to allow it to research, develop and make representations.
- The Parliament and Executive Government should seek representations in writing from the Voice early in the development of proposed laws and policies.

B. Will be chosen by Aboriginal and Torres Strait Islander people based on the wishes of local communities

- Members of the Voice would be selected by Aboriginal and Torres Strait Islander communities, not appointed by the Executive Government.

- Members would serve on the Voice for a fixed period of time, to ensure regular accountability to their communities.
- To ensure cultural legitimacy, the way that members of the Voice are chosen would suit the wishes of local communities and would be determined through the postreferendum process.

C. Will be representative of Aboriginal and Torres Strait Islander communities, gender balanced and include youth

- Members of the Voice would be Aboriginal and/or Torres Strait Islander, according to the standard three part test.
- Members would be chosen from each of the states, territories and the Torres Strait Islands.
- The Voice would have specific remote representatives as well as representation for the mainland Torres Strait Islander population.
- The Voice will have balanced gender representation at the national level.

D. Will be empowering, community-led, inclusive, respectful and culturally informed

- Members of the voice would be expected to connect with – and reflect the wishes of – their communities.
- The Voice would consult with grassroots communities and regional entities to ensure its representations are informed by their experience, including the experience of those who have been historically excluded from participation.

E. Will be accountable and transparent

- The Voice would be subject to standard governance and reporting requirements to ensure transparency and accountability.
- Voice members would fall within the scope of the National Anti-Corruption Commission.
- Voice members would be able to be sanctioned or removed for serious misconduct.

F. Will work alongside existing organisations and traditional structures
- The Voice would respect the work of existing organisations.

G. Will not have a program delivery function
- The Voice would be able to make representations about improving programs and services, but it would not manage money or deliver services.

H. Will not have a veto power

Post-Referendum Process
After the referendum, there will be a process with Aboriginal and Torres Strait Islander communities, the Parliament, and the broader public to settle the Voice design. Legislation to establish the Voice will then go through standard parliamentary processes to ensure adequate scrutiny by elected representatives in both houses of Parliament.

∞∞∞

These principles may be expanded upon through the parliamentary process and will be available to all Australians before they vote at the referendum.

Would the Voice be able to interfere in matters that aren't obviously affecting Indigenous peoples?
The Voice will focus on matters that affect the health and wellbeing of Indigenous peoples.

What powers would a Voice be able to exercise?
The Voice's influence would only be as strong as the quality of its advice based on the views of Aboriginal and Torres Strait Islander peoples across the length and breadth of Australia.

Under this constitutional amendment, future parliaments would be able to make changes to how the Voice would operate, hopefully to improve its relevance and efficiency, as any institution should be able to do. The Parliament could not abolish the Voice, or seriously diminish its ability to make representations on behalf of Aboriginal and Torres Strait Islander peoples, because its existence would be enshrined in the Constitution.

Is it safe to amend the Australian Constitution?

The founding fathers of Australia who wrote the Constitution over 120 years ago clearly understood that it might be necessary to make changes to it from time to time, but they didn't make the Constitution easy to change.

In the case of this referendum, some of the most eminent constitutional experts in the country have carefully analysed the words proposed to be inserted into the Constitution. They have done so to ensure the amendment is true to its intent: constitutional recognition through an advisory Aboriginal and Torres Strait Islander Voice to government and the Parliament.

Some critics have raised concerns that if the Voice can advise the Executive government, as well as the Parliament, High Court challenges might occur that could slow the smooth running of government. Is that a real problem?

Most new policies and laws that pass through the Parliament are first developed by ministers and their departments and approved by the Cabinet. That is at the core of the Executive process.

During the process of Cabinet debate and parliamentary scrutiny, a particular policy might be strengthened, or it might be watered down before it is able to pass through all the stages and gain approval through the final vote in both houses of the Parliament.

If the Voice is to have credibility and be effective on behalf of Indigenous peoples, it will be far more useful for it to make representations to both the Executive and the Parliament. It would make no sense for the Voice to be excluded from any significant part of the policy processes.

On the question of whether access to the Executive could lead to High Court disputes, the former High Court judge and Banking Royal Commissioner, Kenneth Hayne, has some reassuring advice, and he is part of the panel of eminent constitutional experts assisting the government on the referendum.

Kenneth Hayne says it would be a matter for the Voice to decide whether it is appropriate to make representations to Executive Government on a particular policy, and the same would apply to its relationship with the Parliament. But the Voice could not dictate any outcome: it is only advisory. That power to make laws and policies lies with the government and the Parliament.[1]

Section iii of the proposed constitutional amendment also gives Parliament very wide power to legislate all 'matters relating to' the Voice. According to eminent experts like Professor Anne Twomey, this clearly includes being able to legislate to manage how the Voice's representations are treated by government and Parliament. The revised broader wording, released by the Prime Minister in March, makes it even clearer that whether or not advice must be considered by government decision-makers is a matter that can be regulated by Parliament.

Furthermore, the Rule of Law is one of the pillars on which the integrity of our democracy works. It provides a fundamentally important check and balance to ensure that a government or a parliament does not exceed or abuse its power. What is there to fear in that? We should celebrate it.

A sensible government would always want to be seen to at least consider advice from the Voice anyway.

Is it true, as some are claiming, that First Nations sovereignty could somehow be lost by enshrining an Indigenous Voice in the Constitution?

In a word, no. A former Chief Justice of the High Court, Robert French, said it succinctly in a speech in Sydney in February this year:

> *Authority over land and waters within the First Nations legal framework and within the colonising legal framework are capable of co-existence just as common law and traditional law are capable of co-existence of the kind reflected in Native Title agreements. Importantly, constitutional recognition and the creation of the Voice does not involve any ceding of traditional authority over land and waters.[2]*

Hannah McGlade, a Noongah woman who is a member of the United Nations Permanent Forum of Indigenous Peoples, also noted that Indigenous sovereignty cannot be ceded by constitutional recognition. She wrote in an article for *The National Indigenous Times* on 16 January 2023:

> *Nowhere does the Voice to Parliament proposal suggest any agreement of Aboriginal people to cede sovereignty. To the contrary, the proposal recognizes the right of Indigenous people to be heard on laws affecting our people.*

I thought deeply about this concern myself. I concluded that if there is a successful referendum, I, Thomas Mayo, will not wake up the next day and no longer be a Kaurareg Aboriginal and Kalkalgal, Erubamle Torres Strait Islander man.

Why is it that all of the detail about how a Voice will work is not given to the Australian people before we vote in the referendum?

The Australian Constitution does not require or reflect 'details', in the way that 'details' have been called for by the 'No' case in this referendum.

For example, the Constitution grants the Commonwealth the power to impose taxes and laws regarding the collection and administration of taxes, but it does not detail how the Taxation Commissioner is selected, where the tax office will be based, or how much will be spent on tax collection efforts. A similar example is how the Constitution grants the Parliament the power to establish our naval and military defence, but it does not contain the details about how many generals will be appointed, nothing about where military bases should be situated or what resources the government should provide.

The Constitution establishes the institutions and defines the separation of power between the judicial, parliamentary and executive arms of government. It does not establish all of the detail about how things are done.

We elect Parliament to make laws in accordance with the Constitution, and the judicial arm and public opinion, including through media discussion and analysis to guide them and hold them to account.

It will be the same for the Voice to Parliament. How representatives are elected, how many there will be, and from which parts of the country they come, among many other details for such a body, will be decided by the Parliament after the referendum, as is normally done.

Why are some people saying we don't know enough details about the Voice to vote 'Yes' in the referendum?

The 'No' case is asking questions about details that are not matters for the referendum, such as the technicalities of how Indigenous representatives will be elected to the Voice, and what the Voice may make representations on.

Remember, the referendum is only about establishing the principle that Aboriginal and Torres Strait Islander peoples should have a Voice. The rest will be determined by the Parliament.

Throughout the campaign, keep in mind that some people will ask irrelevant questions to give a false impression that there is not enough information for you to make an informed decision. That is why you will hear 'No' case supporters say, 'If you don't know, vote "No".' It might be effective as a simple slogan, but that doesn't make it right.

Is voting in the referendum compulsory?
Yes. All Australians who are eligible to vote are required to vote in the referendum. It is compulsory, just as it is compulsory to vote in a federal, state or territory election.

Do we only need 51 per cent of Australians to vote 'Yes'?
For a referendum to pass, a majority of Australian voters must vote 'Yes'. But we also need a majority of people in a majority of states to vote 'Yes' (four out of six states). This is called a 'double majority'. The Australian Capital Territory (ACT) and the Northern Territory (NT) are not counted as states but their votes contribute to the national vote.

Wouldn't this representative body just add another layer of bureaucracy?
The Aboriginal and Torres Strait Islander Voice would *not* be another layer of bureaucracy. Rather, it would hold the existing bureaucracy to account, and make representations to the government and the Parliament in pursuit of better outcomes for Indigenous peoples and better targeting of government spending.

Some 'No' vote campaigners say that a Voice will divide Australians by race, giving special treatment to Indigenous people. Are they correct?
No. A Voice to Parliament is about recognising Aboriginal and Torres Strait Islander peoples' distinct culture, heritage, history, and their unique connection to the Australian continent that spans over 60,000 years. This would be a force for unity and nation building, rather than division.

A Voice to Parliament would also implement Australia's commitment to the United Nations Declaration on the Right of Indigenous Peoples in domestic law, in particular Article 18, which states:

> *Indigenous peoples have the right to participate in decision-making in matters which would affect their rights, through representatives chosen by themselves in accordance with their own procedures, as well as to maintain and develop their own indigenous decision-making institutions.*

Don't Indigenous peoples already have a voice if they have the right to vote, just like the rest of us?

While it is true that Indigenous peoples have the right to vote now, they are still seriously unrepresented when it comes to influencing the decisions that Parliament makes about them.

While once making up 100 per cent of the population of our continent, Aboriginal and Torres Strait Islander peoples are now less than 4 per cent of the Australian population. They are spread throughout our vast land, across 151 electorates, so their votes have very little influence on who is elected to Parliament or the policies that emanate from it.

There are already eleven Indigenous Members of Parliament, so why do we need an Aboriginal and Torres Strait Islander Voice?

Indigenous politicians necessarily prioritise what the voters in their electorates want, not the specific priorities of Indigenous peoples. If they are members of a political party, they will represent the policies of their party, such as Labor, Liberal, National or the Greens, none of which has a significant number of Indigenous members. The same would apply if they were independents.

Also, while there are eleven Indigenous parliamentarians today, the next election could easily reduce those numbers, based on the mood of electorates, dominated by non-Indigenous voters, for reasons that have nothing to do with the Member of Parliament's Indigenous identity.

By constitutionally enshrining an Aboriginal and Torres Strait Islander Voice, Indigenous peoples will be guaranteed a capacity to make suggestions to the government and the Parliament, whatever the attitude of the government of the day is towards them, and even when there are few or no Indigenous parliamentarians.

As some politicians are saying, why not just legislate the Voice now, so it can prove it is worth doing, before going to a referendum?

It is necessary to hold a referendum to establish a Voice in the Constitution, rather than the Parliament just legislating the Voice, because the principle of listening to Indigenous peoples can only be guaranteed by the will of the Australian people through constitutional recognition. Also, as mentioned above, legislation can be changed, but an amendment to the Constitution will mean the Voice will be ongoing and can't be silenced in the future.

How would the Constitution change if the referendum succeeds?

If the referendum succeeds, the words below are expected to be inserted in a new section in the Constitution. This wording may be changed through the parliamentary process and will be available to all Australians before they vote at the referendum.
(My explanations in italics. TM)

> **Chapter IX: Recognition of Aboriginal and Torres Strait Islander Peoples**
> **129. Aboriginal and Torres Strait Islander Voice**
> In recognition of Aboriginal and Torres Strait Islander peoples as the First Peoples of Australia:
> (i) there shall be a body, to be called the Aboriginal and Torres Strait Islander Voice;

(This sections establishes the requirement for the Parliament to set up the Aboriginal and Torres Strait Islander Voice.)

(ii) the Aboriginal and Torres Strait Islander Voice may make representations to the Parliament and the Executive Government of the Commonwealth on matters relating to Aboriginal and Torres Strait Islander peoples;

(This section establishes that the Voice may express its views to the Parliament and government about Indigenous issues with no right to veto.)

(iii) the Parliament shall, subject to this Constitution, have power to make laws with respect to matters relating to the Aboriginal and Torres Strait Islander Voice, including its composition, functions, powers and procedures.

(This section gives the Parliament the power to make laws relating to the Voice, including how its representations are treated. It provides the flexibility for the Voice to improve with the needs of the people, as all institutions should do. The laws that Parliament makes about the Voice are matters relating to Indigenous peoples, so any changes will be subject to the Voice's advice.)

Have Indigenous peoples been involved in drafting the Voice provision that would be inserted into the Constitution and how the referendum will be held?

Yes. The Albanese government established a Referendum Working Group in 2022. The group is made up of twenty Aboriginal and Torres Strait Islander peoples who have valuable expertise and insights relating to the Voice to Parliament proposal. Its co-chairs are Indigenous Affairs Minister Linda Burney and Senator Patrick Dodson, the government's Special Envoy for Indigenous Reconciliation.

The Referendum Working Group is advising the government on the referendum question, the new provision in the Constitution, and the principles for the Voice. Its aim is to help the referendum succeed in the best way for all Indigenous peoples and for all Australians.

In Appendix 1 we have listed the details of the members of this group, to show the breadth and diversity of their skills and roles.

To support the Referendum Working Group on legal and technical matters, the federal government appointed a panel of constitutional legal experts. Their role is to answer legal questions that come from the Working Group and to advise on the referendum question and the constitutional amendment.

The panel of constitutional legal experts includes:

- Professor Greg Craven AO GCSG
- Professor Megan Davis
- Mr Kenneth Hayne AC KC
- Mr Noel Pearson
- Professor Cheryl Saunders AO
- Professor Anne Twomey AO
- Scientia Professor George Williams AO FASSA
- Professor Asmi Wood.

The government also appointed a Referendum Engagement Group, which is made up of 60 First Nations leaders from around the country (see Appendix 2). This group's role is to provide advice about building community understanding, awareness and support for the referendum.

Is it true, as some people suggest, that Indigenous peoples would have a right to veto legislation by having a third chamber in Parliament?

No. The talk about the Voice being a third chamber in Parliament with special rights is mischievous, much like when Australians were told in the 1990s that Native Title legislation would see people losing their farms and even suburban backyards. It never happened.

Is it true that the Voice will 'govern' Indigenous peoples?

The Voice to Parliament will have no power to govern anyone, including Indigenous peoples. This claim is false.

Why are some Indigenous people not supporting a Voice to Parliament?

Aboriginal and Torres Strait Islander peoples have diverse opinions, just like any other group of people. It would be unrealistic to expect 100 per cent support from over 800,000 people on any matter.

There is no doubt, though, that a majority of Indigenous peoples support a constitutionally enshrined Voice. We know this because of the national consensus reached when the Uluṟu Statement from the Heart was overwhelmingly endorsed after exhaustive community discussions.

Subsequent bipartisan processes involved consultations with Indigenous peoples across the country, in remote, rural and urban communities. In 2018, there was the Joint Select Committee on Constitutional Recognition Relating to Aboriginal and Torres Strait Islander Peoples, co-chaired by Liberal MP Mr Julian Leeser and Labor Senator Patrick Dodson. Then in 2021, the Indigenous Voice Co-design Process, co-chaired by Professor Marcia Langton AO and Professor Tom Calma AO, produced the *Indigenous Voice Co-design Process Final Report to the Australian Government*. Both these processes recorded high levels of Indigenous support.

Polling of Indigenous peoples has been consistent with the results from the previous consultations. The latest poll at the time of writing was an IPSOS poll that found a similar result to Reconciliation Australia's Reconciliation Barometer and CT Group's poll: around 80 per cent of Aboriginal and Torres Strait Islander peoples support a constitutionally enshrined Voice to Parliament.

Why do some Indigenous peoples say they want a Treaty before a Voice?

Each proposal in the Uluru Statement from the Heart – Voice, Treaty and Truth – is as important as the other, and they are presently being advanced by Aboriginal and Torres Strait Islander peoples with local, state and federal governments simultaneously. Following a successful referendum, the federal government would establish a Makarrata Commission to advance both the treaty and truth-telling processes.

Around the country treaty processes have already begun. The treaty process in Victoria is the most advanced, beginning more than ten years ago. Treaty discussions have also commenced in South Australia, Queensland, Tasmania and the Northern Territory. Due to the complexity of treaty making, more than 200 years after first contact, the power imbalance between First peoples and the states, and changes of government and their levels of commitment to reaching a settlement, treaties may take several decades to achieve.

A Voice to Parliament will be integral to the treaty processes in the states and territories because it will provide the means for Aboriginal and Torres Strait Islander peoples to collectively discuss the federal government's responsibilities to the treaties made at the state and territory level. A Voice to Parliament can also achieve positive outcomes in education, health, justice and housing, to name a few examples, without waiting what may be decades for a treaty settlement.

Why do people who argue against a Voice to Parliament say that the government shouldn't waste money on the Voice, they should spend the money on the communities that need it now?

In the absence of a Voice, governments have been wasteful, inconsistent and have failed to close the gap. The Voice will be a means for Aboriginal and Torres Strait Islander peoples in the communities to work closely with governments to better direct funding to where it is needed most and to the greatest possible effect.

A Voice could also highlight government funding decisions that have had positive impacts, while raising accountability when they fail.

If the Voice will only be able to give advice, won't it be too weak to improve the lives of Indigenous peoples? Couldn't a Parliament just ignore the Voice?

The Voice's influence – its power – comes from the capacity it would have to provide well-informed, coherent and transparent representations through those who will be chosen by the Indigenous communities that they will represent.

It is true that a government would not have to accept the Voice's advice. However, a government that spurned credible advice from the Voice without its own credible reasons, would potentially face a harsh judgement at the next election, not just from Indigenous voters but from the millions of non-Indigenous voters who decide to vote 'Yes' to support a Voice at the referendum.

How would a Voice to Parliament benefit all Australians?

Australians have everything to gain and nothing to lose by recognising Indigenous peoples with the fairness of a Voice.

Symbolically, the constitutional recognition of Indigenous peoples would formally unite Australians with the richness of Indigenous culture and heritage. We would become a nation that can boast over 60,000 years of continuous civilisation, walking together with the strength of our diverse backgrounds and cultures.

An Aboriginal and Torres Strait Islander Voice would be of practical and moral benefit to all Australians as well. If there was a Voice to help ensure that funding for programs and services in Indigenous communities is spent more efficiently and effectively, this would not only be good for saving taxpayer dollars, it would simultaneously save and improve Indigenous lives.

OUR CONSTITUTION

(VIA SUCCESSFUL REFERENDUM)

...WOULD PROTECT...

THE PRINCIPLE

THAT INDIGENOUS PEOPLES ARE
RECOGNISED AND CONSULTED
WITH A VOICE TO PARLIAMENT

HISTORY INFORMS US THAT

WITHOUT CONSTITUTIONAL PROTECTION
FUTURE GOVERNMENTS MIGHT WEAKEN OR
ABOLISH THE VOICE ALTOGETHER

**INDIGENOUS VOICES ABOLISHED BY GOVERNMENTS
IN THE PAST:**

NATIONAL ABORIGINAL CONSULTATIVE COMMITTEE
(NACC), ABOLISHED 1977

NATIONAL ABORIGINAL CONFERENCE (NAC),
ABOLISHED 1985

ABORIGINAL AND TORRES STRAIT ISLANDER
COMMISSION (ATSIC), ABOLISHED 2004

NO VOICE = NO IMPROVEMENTS

CHAPTER 6

How the Voice can help to close the gap

PROFESSOR FIONA STANLEY AC AND PROFESSOR MARCIA LANGTON AO

Dr Fiona Stanley AC and Professor Marcia Langton AO, through decades of research and experience, have a deep and clear understanding of how the Voice would help to improve daily life for Indigenous peoples in practical ways. That is why we invited them to share their views in this handbook.

In response, they offer examples of Indigenous-led programs that have, or had, positive impacts for Indigenous peoples. In the development and running of each of these programs, Indigenous peoples speak out and are listened to – they have a voice. The outcomes are practical and often life-changing for the people involved.

ooooo

There is clear evidence that mainstream government services have failed to improve outcomes for Aboriginal and Torres Strait Islander populations, over decades. In fact, there is also evidence that many of these policies cause harm. Take, for example, the Northern Territory Emergency Response initiated by the Howard government in 2007. Known colloquially as the Northern Territory Intervention, it aimed to reduce Indigenous child sexual abuse in response to the *Little Children are Sacred* Report. Instead, it has resulted in increases in child sexual abuse in the Northern Territory every year since then, according to data from the Australian Institute of Health and Welfare (AIHW).

Most state, territory and federal government services for Indigenous peoples have been very expensive, based on inappropriate data and have ignored vital Aboriginal knowledge. However, those programs that are initiated and implemented by Indigenous experts, or in close collaboration with them, are trusted and effectively used by Indigenous communities and organisations. They are based on the local personal, geographic and social circumstances about which Indigenous experts are fully informed, and they enhance the self-esteem and mental health of the community.

Some examples include the First Nations response to Covid, Aboriginal birthing, the Youth Justice System and the Koori Courts. These examples all show that when services for Indigenous peoples are developed with Indigenous knowledge and input, they are extremely effective.

Covid response

All colonised, Indigenous populations around the world are at very high risk from pandemics such as Covid-19. They are more likely to have chronic disease, live in overcrowded housing and are more susceptible to viral infections. Thus, in Australia we expected very high infection, hospitalisations and death rates in Indigenous populations from Covid-19. In fact, Indigenous populations had six times *fewer* cases than non-Indigenous groups, across the whole nation. A complete reversal of the gap! In 2020 and 2021, there were low rates of hospitalisation, no deaths, no cases in remote communities and no cases after the Black Lives Matter marches.

This extraordinary and unexpected outcome was due to Indigenous leadership taking control of all activities for prevention, diagnosis and treatment, as well as housing, social and medical support. From the National Aboriginal Community Controlled Health Organisation (NACCHO) down to state, territory and regional areas, Aboriginal services demanded and received from governments the resources they needed to implement this success. This is a rare instance when authorities listened to Indigenous communities. Think of the potential positive impacts that could come from a Voice being established through constitutional recognition. Comparatively, the 2009 H1N1 flu pandemic was disastrous in Aboriginal populations nationally, and in that case Aboriginal people did not have a seat at the table; in 2020 they did.

Aboriginal birthing

During pregnancy and the early childhood years, all the prerequisites for a healthy, productive life are needed. It is perhaps in the early childhood programs that mainstream services have let down Aboriginal families more than any other, because of the inability of existing programs to help children overcome the effects of colonisation and intergenerational trauma. When Indigenous peoples run their own culturally strong services, however, the outcomes are improved throughout the child's life.

There are two major examples of success here. Studies from around the world and in Australia show that having Aboriginal doulas improves all birth outcomes for babies and their mothers, due to attendance for antenatal care and good preventive and cultural activities. Also, Aboriginal Community Controlled Early Years Centres around Australia (there were 75 centres in 2015) provided culturally safe wrap-around services for parents and children. They adapted all the evidence-based principles of early care to the local Aboriginal settings, and they have resulted in more children being ready for and attending school, more Aboriginal youth completing Year 12 and fewer children with poor mental health (see *Closing the Gap* reports and AIHW research).

The Coalition government stopped funding these 75 centres in 2015/16 with disastrous results, one of which is an increase in youth incarceration.

Youth justice

The developmental pathways that result in more Indigenous children being detained in Australia start in pregnancy and early life. All the children and youth in detention have had a harmful developmental pathway (for example, FASD, ADHD, intellectual disability, early life trauma), and none would have had a normal nurturing early life.

Also, it is worth noting that children can be detained from as young as ten years (the age of criminal responsibility in Australia).

The response of state governments to lock up these damaged children and not provide therapeutic programs results in more leaving detention with very serious behavioural issues. They are much more likely to reoffend and to commit more serious crimes. In addition to the Aboriginal Community Controlled Early Childhood Centres already mentioned, there are several successful Aboriginal diversionary programs that manage these children to avoid them being locked up.

Such programs use strong cultural environments and respected leaders, and they are all regarded as successful, as most of their children avoid incarceration. Many of the Indigenous programs put these damaged children on a pathway to successful societal participation, surrounding them with the strong nurturing and therapeutic services they need. They are much more cost-effective than youth detention centres, which cost around $500,000 per annum per child. Even though underfunded, these Indigenous-run diversionary programs have succeeded in averting catastrophic outcomes for many Aboriginal children.

Koori Courts

The Koori Courts, established in 2002, are a radical departure from the typical Magistrates and County Courts that implement the legal system with a view to imposing a punishment on offenders for committing crimes. The matters before the Koori Courts are largely violence-related, including family violence. Their purpose is to provide a therapeutic style of justice that encourages people not to re-offend. They involve the Aboriginal community, particularly suitable Elders, to achieve better outcomes from the court system when offenders require more than punishment to enable them to behave in socially acceptable ways.

The outstanding feature of the Koori Courts is the service given to the courts by Elders. They are appointed to serve with the presiding magistrate to hear cases, counsel offenders and victims, offer advice on support services, and identify solutions beyond mere punishment to gain longer term beneficial outcomes for perpetrators, victims and the wider community.

A Court Officer in Victoria, speaking about her experience with the Koori Court, said:

[It works] because it's actually giving a chance for the Indigenous people to have a voice. It gives a chance for our Elders to give the people who are coming through the courts the chance to put their point of view … growing up, being an Aboriginal person, you're taught to respect your Elders, and having the Elders on the court makes a big difference to know that you'll be able to express yourself and not only have a conversation with the magistrate but also have conversations with the Elders.[1]

ooooo

As well as these Australian examples, data from Canada has shown that those First Nations populations that run their own services (health, education, welfare, etc.) not only have better services but the rates of youth suicide are much lower.[2] This is due to the high self-esteem of the whole community; they are proud of their culture and their knowledge. Aboriginal birthing services in the Nunavit community in Northern Ontario also showed reduced alcohol use, domestic violence and suicide.[3]

The evidence is clear that having a Voice – that is, a say in issues and programs that affect them – makes a huge difference to improving daily life for First Nations people, from the time of their birth onwards.

FIRST NATIONS PEOPLE

↓

MAKE UP 3.2%
OF THE AUSTRALIAN POPULATION

YET WE ARE
12.5 TIMES
MORE LIKELY TO BE IMPRISONED AS AN ADULT

26 TIMES
MORE LIKELY TO BE IMPRISONED AS A CHILD
COMPARED WITH NON-INDIGENOUS AUSTRALIANS

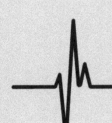
OUR MORTALITY RATE IS
1.7 TIMES HIGHER

WITH
61% DEATHS
BEFORE AGE 65

*COMPARED WITH 17% FOR NON-INDIGENOUS
AUSTRALIANS*

tatistics sourced from Australian Law Reform Commission and Australian Institute of Health and Welfare

CHAPTER 7

How you can help

THOMAS MAYO

When I carried the Uluṟu Statement from the Heart canvas around the country, and now, as I work on the 'Yes' campaign for the referendum, the question I hear most frequently is: 'How can I help?'

My answer goes beyond just asking people to vote 'Yes'. If we want this referendum to succeed, we need you to work as hard as Indigenous peoples did to create this once-in-generations opportunity.

The greatest way you can help is by speaking with your fellow Australians – your family, friends, colleagues and neighbours. Hear them out, show them the respect you'd like them to show you, and always keep your message simple: the change we will say 'Yes' to is safe yet crucial to improving the lives of Indigenous peoples – we are voting 'Yes' to recognition and fairness.

Your most powerful tool is your care, compassion and knowledge. Use these strengths. Show your fellow Australians that hope is greater than hopelessness. Quell any fears.

You need not wait for further invitations or instructions.

Don't hesitate to apply your own initiative and creativity to connect with more people. Be active for the 'Yes' campaign at gatherings around kitchen tables, at barbecues, book clubs, sporting events, schools and at every other opportunity between now and the referendum.

Wear a 'Yes' T-shirt if you like. You may choose to door knock, work at a market stall or polling booth with the 'Yes' campaign, as an official volunteer.

There are many tools for supporters available through the 'Yes' campaign website. You'll find QR codes and website links in the following pages.

I'll help you to get started with some simple advice.

Conversations will make all the difference

1. Start by talking to the people closest to you about why you will vote 'Yes' in the referendum.

2. Listen to the person you are speaking with, rather than talking at them. Ask open questions to explore their position, and where you can, find common ground. Importantly, share the reasons why you have decided to vote 'Yes'.

3. Make a plan about who you will have conversations with and in what order. This way you can measure and expand your reach over the coming months.

4. As you have more conversations, you'll notice that you will express your points more easily and with greater confidence, your narrative will become more settled, and your discussion will become more effective.

5. Aim to talk to a wide variety of people. You don't only have to target those people you think are likely to vote 'No'; also have conversations with people who you think will vote 'Yes' or are undecided.

6. Invite people who will vote 'Yes' to become involved. You may ask them to commit to having conversations with their circle of influence too; and you can invite them to join the campaign as a volunteer.

7. Keep in mind that people are unlikely to change their views if you seek to 'correct' them, regardless of how much they like and respect you. Hear them out and use logic, commonsense and your own story to explain why you will vote 'Yes', and why they might vote 'Yes' too.

8. Remember that the goal of your conversation is to encourage someone to vote 'Yes', and to become involved in the campaign. It is not the time to be correcting a person's language if they are not quite politically correct.

9. If a person you are engaging with is entrenched as a 'No' voter, or if they are being disrespectful or offensive, move on.

10. If you are engaging with an Indigenous person who does not support the Voice to Parliament, accept and respect that some

Indigenous people will not vote 'Yes', and move on, with the confidence that a great majority of us will.

11. Check in on fellow supporters. The road to recognition will have many trolls who will try to intimidate and scare you. Let's look after each other's mental health. We are walking this path to a better future together.

A printable conversation guide is available at: yes23.com.au/resources

Officially join the 'Yes' campaign

The 'Yes' campaign website – yes23.com.au or use the QR code below – has information, campaign tools and a merchandise shop for supporters. It is also the place to register as a supporter or volunteer to keep updated about opportunities to become involved. You can explore the page and take the initiative.

Together Yes

The Together Yes movement aims to enable thousands of people across the country to participate in Kitchen Table Conversations. These discussions are built on respect, safety, listening and learning. They are a simple and practical way for people to come together in their homes or communal spaces and take part in discussions that can lead to a deeper understanding of the issues involved.

We want to see an unprecedented number of Australians taking up the opportunity to be Conversation hosts. I encourage you to urgently share the Together Yes information with anyone who you think might be willing to join us. The months between now and the day of the referendum will go quickly, and time is running out.

You can learn more about the Together Yes movement here or visit togetheryes.com.au:

Workplace and community engagement

Many workplaces, city councils and unions around the country have committed to creating opportunities to engage with the Uluṟu Statement from the Heart and the history and context in which this referendum is being held.

If your workplace hasn't made this commitment yet, I encourage you to explore ways in which your organisation might consider supporting the 'Yes' campaign.

Endnotes

The creation of the Uluru Statement from the Heart
1 *Final Report of the Referendum Council*, 30 June 2017, p. 10.
www.referendumcouncil.org.au

What the Voice means to me *Thomas Mayo*
1 https://rectas.com.au/from-our-heart-to-yours

What the Voice means to me *Kerry O'Brien*
1 ATNS (Agreements, Treaties and Negotiated Settlements), University of
Melbourne. www.atns.net.au
2 Noel Pearson, 'Declaration of Australia and the Australian People', Cape York
Institute, 2 June 2018.
3 *The Guardian*, 3 February 2023.

The history of struggle for an effective Voice
1 Jonathan Richards, *The Secret War: A True History of Queensland's Native Police*,
UQP, 2008..
2 D Bates, *The Passing of the Aborigines*, John Murray, London, 1944.
3 Robert Manne, 'Sorry Business', *The Monthly*, March 2008.
4 P Bartrop, P. (2001). 'The Holocaust, the Aborigines, and the bureaucracy of
destruction: an Australian dimension of genocide', *Journal of Genocide Research*, 3
(1), 2001, p. 75.
5 J W Bleakley, *The Aborigines of Australia*, Jacaranda Press, 1961, p. 164.
6 Rosalind Kidd, *Hard Labour, Stolen Wages: National Report on Stolen Wages*,
Australians for Native Title and Reconciliation (ANTaR), 2007.
7 NSW Public Service Commission, *Everyone's Business*, chapter 6.
8 National Film and Sound Archive.
9 *The 1938 Day of Mourning*, IATSIS.
10 'Nicky Winmar's Stand', *Defining Moments*, National Museum of Australia.
www.nma.gov.au/defining-moments/resources/nicky-winmars-stand
11 Tony Stephens, *Sydney Morning Herald*, 14 February 2015.
12 Gary Foley, 'Harold Holt's death and why the 1967 referendum failed Indigenous
people', *The Guardian*, May 2017.
13 Ibid.
14 Ibid.

15 Barrie Dexter, *Pandora's Box: The Council for Aboriginal Affairs 1967–76*, edited by Gary Foley and Edwina Howell, Keeaira Press, 2015.

16 Gary Foley, 'Harold Holt's death and why the 1967 referendum failed Indigenous people', *The Guardian*, May 2017.

17 Mungo MacCallum, *Crikey*, February 2009.

18 Gough Whitlam, *The Whitlam Government*, Penguin, 1985, p. 468.

19 Paul Keating, Lowitja O'Donoghue Oration, Adelaide, 21 May 2011.

20 Noel Pearson, *Griffith Review*, May 2007.

21 John Howard, *Lazarus Rising*, HarperCollins, 2010.

22 Ibid.

23 Kerrie O'Brien, *Kerry O'Brien: A Memoir*, Allen & Unwin, 2018, pp 452–453.

24 *In the Hands of the Region Report*, November 2003.

25 *The Age*, 5 April 2004.

26 Ibid.

The Voice is about who we are as Australians

1 Gerald Horne, *The Dawning of the Apocalypse*, NYU Press, 2020.

2 Grace Karskens, *People of the River*, Allen & Unwin, 2020, p. 109.

3 https://newsroom.unsw.edu.au/news/business-law/
its-time-walk-together-towards-referendum-indigenous-law-centre

What is a referendum?

1 Gough Whitlam, *The Whitlam Government 1972–1975*, p. 463.

Why vote 'Yes' and other frequently asked questions

1 Justice Kenneth Hayne AC in correspondence with KOB.

2 The Honourable Robert French AC, Former Chief Justice of the High Court of Australia, speaking in the session 'The Evolution of Public Law', 2023 Constitutional Law Online Conference, 10 February 2023.

How the Voice will help to close the gap

1 M Langton, K Smith, T Eastman, L O'Neill, E Cheeseman and M Rose (2020). *Improving family violence legal and support services for Aboriginal and Torres Strait Islander women* (Research report, 25/2020). Transcripts 2019: 994. Sydney: ANROWS.

2 M Chandler and C Lalonde, 'Cultural Continuity as a Protective Factor against Suicide in First Nations Youth', *Horizons – A Special Issue on Aboriginal Youth, Hope or Heartbreak: Aboriginal Youth and Canada's Future*. (10) 2008, pp 68–72.

3 Documentary film *Birth Rites*, written by Jennifer Gherardi and Linda Rawlings; directed by Jennifer Gherardi, 2002.

Further reading

To read more about the 1967 referendum
https://aiatsis.gov.au/explore/1967-referendum

Bain Attwood and Andrew Markus, *The 1967 Referendum: Race, power and the Australian Constitution*, Aboriginal Studies Press, 2007

To read more about the First Nations activism movement of the 1920s and 1930s
Bain Atwood and Andrew Markus, *Thinking Black*, Australian Institute of Aboriginal and Torres Strait Islander Studies, 2004

John Maynard, *Fight for Liberty and Freedom: The origins of Australian Aboriginal activism*, Aboriginal Studies Press, 2007

To read more about the *Mabo* case
Sean Flood, *Mabo: A symbol of struggle: the unfinished quest for Voice Treaty Truth*, Fink Consultancy, c1993

To read more about the Uluṟu Statement from the Heart
Pat Anderson AO and Mark Leibler AC, *Referendum Council Final Report*, 30 June 2017
www.referendumcouncil.org.au/sites/default/files/report_attachments/ Referendum_Council_Final_Report.pdf

Megan Davis and George Williams, *Everything you need to know about the Uluṟu Statement from the Heart*, UNSW Press, 2021

Pat Dodson and Julian Leeser, *Joint Select Committee on Constitutional Recognition Relating to Aboriginal and Torres Strait Islander Peoples Final Report*, 29 November 2018

Professor Marcia Langton AO and Professor Tom Calma AO, *Indigenous Voice Co-Design Process – Final Report to the Australian Government*, July 2021

Thomas Mayo, *Finding the Heart of the Nation: The Journey of the Uluṟu Statement towards Voice, Treaty and Truth*, 2nd edition, Hardie Grant Explore, 2022

Thomas Mayo, 'Where Truths Collide: Challenging Australia's shaky foundations', *Griffith Review Online*

Thomas Mayo, 'When the Heart Speaks: Learning the language of listening', *Griffith Review Online*

Thomas Mayo, 'A Dream that cannot be Denied: On the road to Freedom Day', *Griffith Review Online*

Thomas Mayo, Blak Douglas (illustrator), *Finding Our Heart: The story about the Uluru Statement for Young Australians*, Hardie Grant Explore, 2022

Shireen Morris and Damien Freeman, *Statements from the Soul: The Moral Case for the Uluru Statement from the Heart*, La Trobe University Press, 2023

Adam Phelan, 'It's time to walk together towards a referendum': Indigenous Law Centre, 2 March 2021

Teela Reid, Contributing Editor, Ashley Hay, Editor, *Griffith Review: Acts of Reckoning,* Edition 76, April 2022

To read more about the Gurindji Wave Hill Walk-Off
Rosie Smiler and Thomas Mayo, *Freedom Day: Vincent Lingiari and the story of the Wave Hill Walk-Off*, Hardie Grant Explore, 2021

Charlie Ward, *A Handful of Sand: The Gurindji Struggle, After the Walk-Off*, Monash University Publishing, 2016

See also
Gerald Horne, *The Dawning of the Apocalypse*, Monthly Review Press, New York, 2020

Grace Karskens, *People of the River*, Allen & Unwin, Sydney, 2020

Rosalind Kidd, *Hard Labour, Stolen Wages: National Report on Stolen Wages*, Australians for Native Title and Reconciliation, 2007

Robert Manne, 'Sorry Business', *The Monthly*, March 2008

Kerry O'Brien, *Keating*, Allen & Unwin, 2016

Kerry O'Brien, *Kerry O'Brien: A Memoir*, Allen & Unwin, 2018

Noel Pearson, 'Declaration of Australia and the Australian People', Cape York Institute, 2 June 2018

Noel Pearson, *Mission: Essays, Speeches, Ideas,* Black Inc., 2021.

Jonathan Richards, *The Secret War: A True History of Queensland's Native Police*, UQP, 2008

Gough Whitlam, *The Whitlam Government 1972–1975*, Penguin Books, 1985

Referendum Working Group

Co-chairs: Hon Linda Burney MP, Minister for Indigenous Australians; Senator Patrick Dodson, Chair of Joint Standing Committee on Aboriginal and Torres Strait Islander Affairs

- Mr Dale Agius
  Commissioner for First Nations Voice, SA

- Ms Pat Anderson AO
  Co-chair of Uluru Dialogue
  Chair, Batchelor Institute

- Ms Geraldine Atkinson
  Co-chair, First Peoples' Assembly of Victoria
  Member of Indigenous Voice Co-design Groups

- Professor Tom Calma AO
  Co-chair, Indigenous Voice Co-design Groups
  Chancellor, University of Canberra
  Co-chair, Reconciliation Australia

- Professor Megan Davis
  Co-chair of Uluru Dialogue
  Balnaves Chair in Constitutional Law and Pro Vice-Chancellor
  Indigenous, UNSW

- Mr Rodney Dillon
  Chair, Tasmanian Aboriginal Heritage Council
  Co-chair, Tasmanian Regional Aboriginal Community Alliance

- Mr Sean Gordon
  Managing Director, Gidgee Group
  Councillor, University of Newcastle

- Dr Jackie Huggins AM FAHA
  Co-chair, Treaty Advancement Committee, QLD
  Co-chair, National Apology Foundation

- Professor Marcia Langton AO
  Co-chair, Indigenous Voice Co-design Groups
  Associate Provost, University of Melbourne

- Mr Thomas Mayo
  National Indigenous Officer, Maritime Union of Australia
  Board member, Australians for Indigenous Constitutional Recognition

- Mr Tony McAvoy SC
  Acting Treaty Commissioner, NT
  Barrister

- Ms June Oscar AO
  Aboriginal and Torres Strait Islander Social Justice Commissioner

- Mr Dean Parkin
  Director, From the Heart

- Mr Noel Pearson
  Founder, Cape York Institute
  Advisor, From the Heart
  Member of Indigenous Voice Co-design Groups

- Ms Sally Scales
  Member of Uluru Dialogue
  APY Artist

- Mr Napau Pedro Stephen AM
  Chair, Torres Strait Regional Authority

- Mr Marcus Stewart
  Co-chair, First Peoples' Assembly of Victoria
  Member of Indigenous Voice Co-design Groups

- Ms Pat Turner AM
  Lead Convenor of Coalition of Peaks
  CEO, National Aboriginal Community Controlled Health Organisation
  Member of Indigenous Voice Co-design groups

- Hon Ken Wyatt AM
  Former Minister for Indigenous Australians

- Professor Peter Yu AM
  Vice-President (First Nations), ANU
  Member of Indigenous Voice Co-design Groups

- Dr Galarrwuy Yunupingu AM
  Foundation Chair, Yothu Yindi Foundation
  Member of Indigenous Voice Co-design Groups

Referendum Engagement Group

- Mr Thomas Amagula
  Deputy Chair, Anindilyakwa Land Council

- Mr Richard Ah Mat
  Chair, Cape York Land Council

- Cr Ross Andrews
  Mayor, Yarrabah Aboriginal Shire Council
  Australian Local Government Association representative
  Member of Indigenous Voice Co-design Groups

- Mr Nathan Appo
  Institute of Urban Indigenous Health

- Professor Muriel Bamblett AO
  CEO, Victorian Aboriginal Child Care Agency
  Coalition of Peaks representative

- Ms Jennifer Beale
  CEO, Butucarbin Aboriginal Corporation

- Professor Jack Beetson
  Australian Centre for Agriculture and Law, University of New England

- Mr Dameyon Bonson
  Founder, Black Rainbow Living Well

- Ms Wendy Brabham
  Deputy Chair, Wathaurong Aboriginal Co-operative

- Mr Paul Briggs OAM
  Executive Chair, Kaiela Institute

- Mr Gavin Brown
  Co-CEO, PwC Indigenous Consulting

- Mr Selwyn Button
  Chair, The Lowitja Institute

- Mr Nicholas Cameron
  Tasmanian Regional Aboriginal Communities Alliance
  Chair, Melythina Tiakana Warrana Aboriginal Corporation

- Ms Shirleen Campbell
  Co-cordinator, Tangentyere Women's Family Safety Group

- Cr Danny Chapman
  Chair, NSW Aboriginal Land Council

- Ms Fiona Cornforth
  CEO, The Healing Foundation

- Dr Josie Douglas
  General Manager Health Services Division, Central Australian
  Aboriginal Congress

- Ms Katrina Fanning AO PSM
  Director, Coolamon Advisors
  Member of Indigenous Voice Co-design Groups

- Mr Tyronne Garstone
  CEO, Kimberley Land Council
  Advisor, From the Heart

- Mr Mick Gooda
  Co-chair, QLD Treaty Advancement Committee
  Member of Indigenous Voice Co-design Groups

- Mr Damian Griffis
  CEO of First Peoples Disability Network Australia
  Member of Indigenous Voice Co-design Groups

- Ms Tanya Hosch
  Executive General Manager, Inclusion & Social Policy, AFL
  Advisor, From the Heart

- Mr Paul House
  Senior Community Engagement Officer, ANU First Nations Portfolio
  Board member, Ngambri Local Aboriginal Land Council
  Member of Indigenous Voice Co-design Groups

- Mr Gibson Farmer Illortaminni
  Chair, Tiwi Land Council

- Ms Deborah Katona
  Senior Manager Policy, Northern Land Council

- Cr Esma Livermore
  Deputy Mayor, Queanbeyan-Palerang Regional Council
  Australian Local Government Association representative

- Mr Jamie Lowe
  CEO, National Native Title Council
  Member of Indigenous Voice Co-design Groups

- Dr Hannah McGlade
  Associate Professor, Curtin Law School

- Mr Wayne Miller
  CEO, Ceduna Aboriginal Corporation
  Chair, Far West Community Leadership Group
  Member of Indigenous Voice Co-design groups

- Cr Phillemon Mosby
  Mayor, Torres Strait Island Regional Council
  Australian Local Government Association representative

- Mr Kado Muir
  Activist & Impact Entrepreneur, Dilji
  Social Anthropologist

- Ms Karen Mundine
  CEO, Reconciliation Australia
  Advisor, From the Heart

- Ms Teela Reid
  Uluṟu Dialogue Group
  Lawyer, University of Sydney Law School

- Cr Matthew Ryan
  Mayor, West Arnhem Regional Council
  Australian Local Government Association representative

- Mr Shane Sturgiss
  CEO, BlaQ Aboriginal Corporation

- Mr Ian Trust AO
  National Chair, Empowered Communities
  Executive Chair, Wunan Foundation

- Mr Lesley Turner
  CEO, Central Land Council

- Mr Richard Weston
  Deputy Children's Guardian for Aboriginal Children and Young People, NSW
  Member of Indigenous Voice Co-design Groups

- Mr Sammy Wilson
  Traditional Owner, Uluṟu
  Former Chair, Central Land Council

- Mr Scott Wilson
  Lead Convenor of SA Aboriginal Community Controlled Network
  Coalition of Peaks representative

- Professor Asmi Wood
  Professor, ANU College of Law

About the authors

Thomas Mayo is a Torres Strait Islander man born on Larrakia country in Darwin. As an Islander growing up on the mainland, he learned to hunt traditional foods with his father and to island dance from the Darwin community of Torres Strait Islanders. In high school, Thomas' English teacher suggested he should become a writer. He didn't think then that he would become one of the first Torres Strait Islander authors to have a book published for the general trade. Instead, he became a wharf labourer from the age of seventeen, until he became a union official for the Maritime Union of Australia in his early thirties. Quietly spoken in character, Thomas found his voice on the wharves. As he gained the skills of negotiation and organising in the union movement, he applied those skills to advancing the rights of Indigenous peoples, becoming a signatory to the Uluru Statement from the Heart and a tireless campaigner. At the Uluru National Constitutional Convention, Thomas delivered a speech immediately before the Uluru Statement was read for the first time and was subsequently endorsed to standing acclamation. Following the Convention, Thomas was entrusted to carry the sacred canvas of the Uluru Statement from the Heart. He then embarked on an eighteen-month journey around the country to garner support for a constitutionally enshrined First Nations Voice, and a Makarrata Commission for truth-telling and agreement-making or treaties. Through to the Voice referendum in late 2023, Thomas has not stopped crisscrossing the Australian continent, speaking with tens of thousands of Australians, encouraging them to vote 'Yes'.

Thomas is the author of six books, including the first and second editions of *Finding The Heart of The Nation*, *Dear Son* and the children's books – *Finding Our Heart* and *Freedom Day*.

Kerry O'Brien is a multi-award winning journalist and author who rose to prominence through such trail-blazing ABC programs as *This Day Tonight*, *Four Corners*, *7.30* and *Lateline*. He was also the Seven Network's first US correspondent. Kerry was press secretary to Labor leader Gough Whitlam in Opposition.

He served on the Eminent Persons Panel advising the Queensland Government on a pathway to treaty with Indigenous Queenslanders and a process of historic truth-telling. The panel's recommendations have since been legislated. Kerry has honorary doctorates with the University of Queensland and the Queensland University of Technology and has written a best-selling biography on Paul Keating and a memoir. Kerry has also served as Chair of the Walkley Foundation.

Professor Fiona Stanley AC FAA FASSA is a vocal advocate for the needs of children and their families. She was the founding Director of the Telethon Kids Institute, established in Perth in 1990, and is now the Institute's Patron, where she continues to advocate for the Institute and the welfare of families. Professor Stanley is also a distinguished Professorial Fellow in the School of Paediatrics and Child Health at the University of Western Australia. She was named Australian of the Year in 2003, and she is the UNICEF Australian Ambassador for Early Childhood Development.

Professor Marcia Langton AO PhD Macq U, BA (Hons) ANU, FASSA is one of Australia's most important voices for Indigenous Australia. As an anthropologist and geographer, she has made a significant contribution to government and non-government policy as well as to Indigenous studies, Native Title and resource management, art and culture, and women's rights. Professor Langton has held the Foundation Chair of Australian Indigenous Studies at the University of Melbourne since February 2000. In 2016, she was honoured as a Redmond Barry Distinguished Professor, and was then appointed as the first Associate Provost at the University of Melbourne in 2017. She has received many other accolades, including the Officer of the Order of Australia award in 2020.